2009 NPS Ocean and Coastal Park Workshop Results and Proceedings

Establishing a Community of Practice, Formulating Guidance and Charting a Course for the Future

Natural Resource Report NPS/NRPC/WRD/NRR—2010/194

Julia F. Brunner
Geologic Resources Division
Natural Resource Program Center
National Park Service
P.O. Box 25287
Denver, CO 80225

Jeffrey N. Cross
Water Resources Division
Natural Resource Program Center
National Park Service
1201 Oakridge Drive, Suite 250
Fort Collins, CO 80525

May 2010

U.S. Department of the Interior
National Park Service
Natural Resource Program Center
Fort Collins, Colorado

The National Park Service, Natural Resource Program Center publishes a range of reports that address natural resource topics of interest and applicability to a broad audience in the National Park Service and others in natural resource management, including scientists, conservation and environmental constituencies, and the public.

The Natural Resource Report Series is used to disseminate high-priority, current natural resource management information with managerial application. The series targets a general, diverse audience, and may contain NPS policy considerations or address sensitive issues of management applicability.

All manuscripts in the series receive the appropriate level of peer review to ensure that the information is scientifically credible, technically accurate, appropriately written for the intended audience, and designed and published in a professional manner. This report received informal peer review by subject-matter experts who were not directly involved in the collection, analysis, or reporting of the data.

Views, statements, findings, conclusions, recommendations, and data in this report are those of the author(s) and do not necessarily reflect views and policies of the National Park Service, U.S. Department of the Interior. Mention of trade names or commercial products does not constitute endorsement or recommendation for use by the National Park Service.

This report is available from the Geologic Resources Division (http://inside.nps.gov/waso/waso.cfm?prg=740&lv=4) and the Water Resources Division (http://www.nature.nps.gov/water/wrdpub.cfm), as well as the Natural Resource Publications Management website (http://www.nature.nps.gov/publications/NRPM).

Please cite this publication as:

Brunner, J. F., and J. N. Cross. 2010. 2009 NPS ocean and coastal park workshop results and proceedings: establishing a community of practice, formulating guidance and charting a course for the future. Natural Resource Report NPS/NRPC/WRD/NRR—2010/194. National Park Service, Fort Collins, Colorado.

NPS 999/102099, May 2010

CONTENTS

Introduction

The NPS Natural Resource Program Center's Geologic Resources and Water Resources Divisions hosted a three-day facilitated workshop attended by 53 resource managers and staff from ocean, coastal, and Great Lakes parks, regional offices, and central offices throughout the National Park System. The workshop, entitled "Establishing a Community of Practice, Formulating Guidance, and Charting a Course for the Future," was held in Boulder, Colorado on August 25-27, 2009. The purpose of the workshop was to carry out three tasks identified in the National Park Service national and regional ocean stewardship strategies: (1) analyze NPS authorities, (3) identify NPS responsibilities and opportunities, and (3) improve communication among ocean professionals.

The workshop provided a forum for representatives from ocean and coastal parks and regions to share expertise and experiences addressing ocean/coastal legal, policy, and resource management topics; explore existing approaches to resource management and ongoing needs; and offer recommendations for improved NPS ocean and coastal park stewardship.

Prior to the workshop, participants identified the following topics as their highest priorities:

1. climate change;

2. fisheries management and other extractive uses;

3. aquatic invasive species;

4. pollution, water quality, and watershed management;

5. sediment management and coastal infrastructure; and

6. habitat and ecosystem restoration.

Because climate change was identified by most workshop participants as a high-priority topic, the workshop organizers and facilitators decided that this topic should not be addressed separately, but instead should be incorporated into the five other high priority topics as the driver for maintaining biodiversity, natural processes, and ecosystem resilience.

Day One of the workshop was a plenary session during which workshop participants gave brief presentations on each of the five remaining high priority topics, followed by group discussion, questions, and comments. On Days Two and Three, the participants divided into five breakout groups. Breakout groups analyzed the topics and possible solutions, reported on their progress in plenary sessions on Days Two and Three, and then revised their recommendations based on the feedback received from the other participants. The final plenary session on Day Three identified cross-cutting issues and tools, suggested priorities, and addressed NPS ocean and coastal budget needs.

The next section (Summary of Workshop Results and Recommendations) distills the three days of workshop proceedings into a concise list of priority actions and topic-specific recommendations to guide the direction and action items for the NPS oceans and coastal program.

The appendices summarize the workshop. Appendix A contains a list of the participants. Appendix B describes the workshop planning, budget, and agendas. Appendix C contains the workshop proceedings.

In the short term, the Natural Resource Program Center (NRPC) will use the information in this report to develop a briefing for NPS management on the needs and recommendations from the workshop participants, who represented nearly 30 park units, five regional offices, and several central offices, and who cumulatively possess a wealth of experience in managing ocean and Great Lakes park units. In the long term, the NRPC ocean and coastal program managers will use this document as an ongoing reminder of park needs, which will help us with project formulation, staffing decisions, and partnership efforts.

Summary of Workshop Results and Recommendations

Overarching Recommendations

The recommendations made by the workshop participants over the course of the three days contained both general and topic-specific suggestions. Overall, the top priorities were:

1. Improve Internal Communication: The NPS needs to enhance the NPS oceans and Great Lakes "community of practice." This could be accomplished via a Website managed by the Natural Resource Program Center that contains ocean-related scientific, technical, and policy information, such as articles and briefings. Webinars could be used improve communication on significant resource issues.

2. Develop Baseline Inventories and Information: The NPS needs to continue to cooperatively develop benthic habitat inventories and collect other baseline information on coastal processes, resources, and infrastructure to help parks measure the impacts of climate change and increase parks resilience.

3. Determine and Disseminate Information about NPS Jurisdiction and Regulatory Authorities: The NPS needs to continue researching and developing an NPS jurisdiction handbook and engaging with attorneys in the DOI Office of the Solicitor to establish a servicewide understanding of NPS authorities in ocean and coastal park units.

4. Develop an Ocean and Coastal Management Director's Order: The NPS needs to develop a Director's Order to stimulate and endorse the multiplicity of efforts to protect ocean and coastal park resources. This document should:

   - confirm that NPS Management Policies apply to marine and coastal resources,

   - reduce or eliminate the disparity between the protection afforded to marine and terrestrial areas,

   - contain guidance for managing coastal ecosystems and processes to increase their resilience, and mitigate the causes and adapt to the effects of climate change,

   - direct that best available scientific data must be used for management actions affecting parks,

   - designate all ocean and coastal park waters as Marine Protected Areas and contain guidance for implementing Executive Order 13158, including the establishment of no-take areas within each park unit to serve as standards for protection and as benchmarks for research programs,

   - contain a mechanism for evaluating competing cultural and natural resource projects, and

   - contain a supportive statement regarding park efforts for engaging early and often with all parties and processes affecting marine management.

5. Seek Regulatory and Legislative Revisions: The NPS needs to revise its regulations at 36 C.F.R. Part 2 and possibly promulgate new park-specific regulations to clarify NPS management authorities. The NPS should also discuss with Congress the need for revision of the Clean Water Act to designate all park waters as Tier III waters, the need for periodic adjustment of ocean and coastal park unit boundaries so that these parks continue to include the resources for which the park was established, and the need for amending the Submerged Lands Act to clarify the impacts of sea level rise on state boundaries, federal boundaries, and the boundaries of NPS units.

High Priority Topics: Analysis and Recommendations

At the workshop, each breakout group identified the problems associated with one of the five high priority topics and recommended various solutions including proposed legislative and regulatory revisions, language for an NPS Director's Order or guidance document, working groups, partnerships, or operational changes. These recommendations are summarized below.

1. Fisheries Management and Other Extractive Uses

Submerged natural resources in ocean and coastal parks are not managed in the same way as terrestrial natural resources. Harvest and enhancement are typically allowed in ocean and coastal systems. Parks and fishery management agencies do not always have the same mission and goals (protection vs. harvest), and state agencies focus on stocks rather than fishery resources within park. Some parks do not understand their jurisdiction and authorities. The terms exclusive, concurrent, proprietary, bottomlands, and submerged lands are often confusing. Existing fishery regulations (e.g., bag and size limits, seasons, illegal harvest) are not always enforced (lower priority and shortage of law enforcement rangers).

Current management focuses on stocks, populations, and individual species, not on ecosystems. Legal and illegal harvesting has resulted in population declines that affect NPS ecosystem integrity and resilience to climate change. The indirect effects of fishing (e.g., incidental or bycatch, habitat destruction, derelict fishing gear, lights, etc.) adversely impact NPS resources, ecosystems, and ecosystem services. Influences beyond park boundaries (e.g., energy development, mariculture, fish stocking, etc.) have the potential to adversely impact NPS resources, ecosystems, and ecosystem services. The effects of climate change will exacerbate adverse impacts on NPS resources and create further stress on ecosystem functions. Warming of the oceans will result in changes in the distribution and abundance of species and the formation of new assemblages and relationships. More aggressive management actions (e.g., assisted migration, genetic manipulation for species more adaptable to climate change) may be necessary. Parks need guidance, standards, and strategies to manage fisheries and other submerged natural resources consistent with NPS goals and to increase their resiliency to the impacts of climate change. Cooperation with management partners (i.e., states and fishery management councils) is essential because fish populations extend beyond park boundaries.

Regulatory Revisions. Workshop participants recommended that the NPS seek regulatory revisions in the following areas:

    1.1   Revise 36 C.F.R. § 2.1 and § 2.3 to clarify that these regulations apply regardless of land ownership and whether a park has proprietary, exclusive, or concurrent jurisdiction.

    1.2   Create special regulations to protect species that are not overfished yet.

Director's Order and Reference Manual. Workshop participants recommended that a Director's Order and Reference Manual be created to provide direction and guidance on the following topics:

    1.3   Elevate management of aquatic and marine systems to be comparable with management of terrestrial systems to ensure ocean and coastal ecosystem integrity. Clarify competing objectives – harvest vs. protection – and make "no fishing" the default to achieve parity between hunting and fishing in parks.

    1.4   Develop ecosystem-based management principles and implementation guidance to change the paradigm from managing static locations and single species to managing dynamic ecosystems. Develop guidance for management of species with life cycles that occur outside park boundaries. Parks should manage for resiliency and minimize human intervention, influence, and impacts.

1.5   Clarify the goals, purposes, and permitted and non-permitted activities for NPS marine protected areas (MPAs) and marine reserves. Seek legislation to give MPAs more protections and designate wilderness in ocean and coastal parks.

1.6   Develop national policy to implement and monitor no-take MPAs (undisturbed natural standards) in each unit. Use these areas to determine what unexploited populations, habitats, and ecosystems look like as baseline to measure impacts.

1.7   Define NPS management objectives for fishing management (NPS Management Policies 8.2.2.5); 4.4.1, 4.4.2, and 4.4.3 are too general.

1.8   Develop guidance for parks on the impacts of external aquaculture operations on NPS resources.

Working Groups. Workshop participants recommended establishing working groups to:

1.9   Develop language appropriate for a DO to move from single species/snapshot-in-time-based management to ecosystem-based management and develop principles that reflect management for resiliency in the face of climate change.

Partnerships. Workshop participants recommended that the NPS should strengthen its partnerships and collaboration efforts in the following areas:

1.10   Participate with NOAA MPA Center to nominate all ocean and coastal parks to national list (10 already listed; more to be nominated in fall 2009) and in future MPA gap and threat analyses.

1.11   Encourage states to manage for natural processes and communities and abandon the introduction of and management for nonnative species.

1.12   Participate in existing forums with stakeholder groups, state, and federal agencies on coastal fishery and other issues. Communicate park jurisdiction, legal authority, and treaty rights to stakeholders. Communicate why parks need a higher level of protection than surrounding waters.

1.13   In the absence of clear legal authority or agreement on jurisdiction, temporarily seek common ground with states and others to pursue better stewardship of fisheries. Develop memoranda to accomplish common conservation goals.

1.14   Collaborate with partners and user groups to explore options to protect NPS resources and to expand protection of ecosystem or habitats outside park boundaries.

1.15   Develop and implement interagency agreements to share data, information, and resources (e.g., 2009 NOAA-NPS MOU).

Operations. Workshop participants recommended the following changes to operations:

1.16   Revise funding mechanisms to support ecosystem management and climate change. The PMIS process favors projects that support crisis management, not proactive projects.

1.17   Incorporate ecosystem goals into resource management plans (including fishery management plans) and resource stewardship strategies.

1.18   Increase ecosystem resiliency to address impacts of climate change and increase options for adaptation by restoring coastal and fluvial processes, protecting species not over-fished yet, managing for healthy fish populations.

1.19   Develop regional approaches to implement ecosystem management among parks. Create formal coastal networks of parks (e.g., Colorado River Board, Alaska parks) and develop pilot/case studies among parks/federal agencies/states. Collect data to support science-based ecosystem management.

1.20   Implement and monitor no-take areas in each unit as undisturbed natural standards/controls; identify and monitor key indicators to measure success (e.g. presence of high-level predators, healthy fish populations, biodiversity, etc.).

1.21   Increase law enforcement activities and citations for fisheries violations. Use public outreach via fishery awareness and education courses to increase stewardship of NPS resources.

1.22   Implement fishery-independent monitoring programs.

2. Pollution, Water Quality, and Watershed Management

The waters and associated resources of National Parks are threatened by internal and external sources of pollution. Nutrient enrichment and contaminants are priority issues. Other issues include pathogens, altered salinity, light and sound pollution, marine debris, water clarity, and ocean acidification. Pollution from external and internal sources cause a variety of impacts within parks including algal blooms, hypoxic conditions, fish kills, and change in the structure and function of ecosystems, all of which can degrade visitor experience.

Solutions to water quality problems differ depending on the source. Currently, the U.S. Environmental Protection Agency (USEPA) regulatory process does not adequately protect NPS water quality from external sources of pollution because the criteria for Tier III waters do not recognize park status alone as warranting Tier III protection. Instead, parks must demonstrate that their waters are pristine to be eligible for protected water status. Even then, the Tier III nominations and protection for park waters must be approved by the individual states, which face political pressure to avoid any new restrictions on watershed development and pollution/nutrient inputs. NPS Management Policies in Chapters 3 and 4 are not strong enough to support park efforts to protect water quality from external sources of pollution through cooperative conservation and partnerships.

Control of internal pollution sources requires attention to facilities, such as septic systems, marinas, roads and parking lots, and fuel tanks, and to activities and operations, such as agricultural leases, concessions, landscaping practices, and pesticide use. NPS Management Policies in Chapters 1 and 9 discuss sustainability of park facilities, activities, and operations, but the language is insufficient to protect water quality in coastal parks.

Legislative Revisions. Workshop participants recommended that the NPS seek legislative revisions in the following area:
2.1   Work with USEPA in the amendment of the Clean Water Act to designate ocean and coastal park waters as Tier III protected waters regardless of whether or not those waters are pristine so that anti-degradation protection by the states is mandatory, rather than at the states' discretion.

Regulatory Revisions. Workshop participants recommended that the NPS work with the USEPA to seek these regulatory revisions:
2.2   Tighten Clean Water Act and Coastal Zone Management Act anti-degradation water quality regulations/standards for parks and non-point source programs.

2.3   Develop water quality standards for nitrogen, phosphorous, and emerging contaminants and, under the Clean Air Act, develop air emissions standards for mercury.

2.4   Require notice of NPDES permit actions to all park units/affiliated areas within the watershed/aquifer, improve the state NPDES permit review process to address alternatives so permits focus on impacts to ecological systems and include better treatment options, and create a federal agency appeal process for NPDES permits to USEPA Regional Office of state-delegated permits before permit is finalized.

Working Groups. Workshop participants recommended establishing working groups to:

2.5   Develop guidance for working through the state and federal regulatory system to obtain the highest protection for park waters from external sources of pollution.

2.6   Address coastal park water pollution from park facilities and activities by recommending funding changes to ensure the remediation of in-park facilities and activities known to cause pollution and by issuing guidance directing that existing and new park facilities and activities do not degrade NPS water quality.

Partnerships. Workshop participants recommended that the NPS should strengthen its partnerships and collaboration efforts in the following areas:

2.7   Develop DOI-USEPA MOU at national and regional levels to protect and enhance DOI resource area waters by, for example, improving USEPA Regional Office oversight of state permits affecting parks, and accelerating the pace of state designation of Tier III waters in parks through USEPA's grant, schedules, and oversight processes.

2.8   Develop local/regional level partnerships to cooperatively manage local and park water resources, participate more effectively in the state and federal water quality regulatory processes, and identify important land parcels to protect through conservation easements.

2.9   Work with DOI sister agencies (e.g., USFWS) in legislative and regulatory revision efforts.

2.10   Work with U.S. Coast Guard (USCG) and states to develop geographic response strategies and reduce the incidence of spills. Participate in drills and train for oil spills and prevention.

2.11   Identify impaired waters that negatively affect coastal park water quality. Participate in the TMDL process to bring listed waters into compliance with Clean Water Act standards.

Operations. Workshop participants recommended the following concept for NPS operations:

2.12   Demonstrating to visitors, agencies, and community groups the best management practices that parks use to protect coastal water quality.

2.13   Identify and monitor pollution impacts on coastal park resources.

3. Habitat and Ecosystem Restoration

Coastal and marine habitats and biodiversity in parks are under increasing threats and stress from habitat fragmentation and degradation due to development, watershed alteration, water withdrawal and pollution, and consumptive uses of land and water resources. Climate change is causing additional abrupt and long-term impacts, including sea level rise, lake level change, ocean warming, ocean acidification, intensification of storms, and other phenomena.

Parks are not able to effectively and consistently restore ecosystems to achieve the NPS mandate to conserve parks unimpaired for the enjoyment of current and future generations because of the following reasons: lack of baseline or reference condition information; lack of applied research and monitoring that deters adaptive management and inhibits learning and evaluation of restoration results; many factors or threats affecting park resources emanate from beyond park boundaries and NPS jurisdiction; some state or federal agency missions are inconsistent with NPS mandates; single species recovery goals under the Endangered Species Act conflict with broader habitat or ecological restoration goals; and concerns of local communities and/or park visitors.

In addition, inconsistent servicewide project development and inadequate sources of funding for coastal restoration hinder systematic and effective restoration of ocean and coastal habitats. Lastly, National Environmental Policy Act (NEPA) compliance requirements may not be relevant to changing conditions and/or may exceed project budgets and timelines.

Working Groups. Workshop participants recommended establishing working groups to:

    3.1   Develop policy and scientific guidance for coastal and marine restoration that emphasizes NPS standards and goals, such as natural processes/functions, no net loss of habitat, and the reasons for building resiliency into ecosystems as an effective response to climate change. Policy and guidance should contain management strategies for the following: prevention of vessel groundings; avoiding alteration of natural processes; restoring natural processes and resilience at the park, landscape, and bioregional levels (i.e., watershed integrity, hydrologic characteristics, plant and animal community composition); ensuring that adaptive management is supported by monitoring and applied research is integral to the restoration process; and use of decision trees to guide prioritization of restoration projects within the context of climate change and changes in species ranges and habitat condition.

    3.2   Develop a framework to support servicewide restoration program for coastal and marine ecological restoration.

    3.3   Review NEPA compliance procedures and recommend ways to provide more flexibility and speed for habitat restoration.

Partnerships. Workshop participants recommended that the NPS should strengthen its partnerships and collaboration efforts in the following area:

    3.4   Ecosystem restoration generally.

4. Aquatic Invasive Species

The NPS typically does not, but should, apply the existing NPS Management Policies (Sections 4.4.4, 4.4.4.2, and 4.4.1.3) in the marine environment. There is a lack of systematic guidance and tools to help parks implement these policies. The NPS lacks the scientific basis and scientific capacity, including baseline information (inventory and monitoring), impacts, interactions, and response, which diminishes our credibility. The public is not fully informed of or engaged in the impacts of invasive species on park resources. There is confusion among the NPS and the public about NPS legal mandates and enforcement. For example, the NPS has virtually no regulations about aquatic invasive species in parks. NPS is not as effective as it could be in partnering and collaborating with other entities. Increasing the resiliency of park ecosystem processes would help to prevent and/or reduce new invasions.

Regulatory Revisions. Workshop participants recommended that the NPS should seek these regulatory revisions:

    4.1   Work with the USEPA and/or the U.S. Coast Guard to improve ballast water regulations and include language prohibiting ballast water discharge in or near NPS waters.

    4.2   Because prevention is the best strategy, the NPS should promulgate servicewide regulations, such as live bait restrictions, to prevent the introduction of aquatic invasive species in parks.

Director's Order. Workshop participants recommended that the NPS Ocean and Coastal Management Director's Order should include:

4.3 A specific statement that NPS Management Policies on invasive species should be implemented in ocean and coastal parks.

4.4 A statement that the NPS will conduct and encourage actions that would prevent and/or remove stressors that reduce the resiliency of park resources.

Working Groups. Workshop participants recommended establishing working groups to:

4.5 Develop guidance to help parks bridge the gap between NPS Management Policies and implementation of the policies.

4.6 Incorporate information on invasives into park interpretive programs and other types of outreach to increase a public sense of stewardship, and train volunteers in ocean and coastal resources, including recognition and reporting of invasive species.

Partnerships. Workshop participants recommended that the NPS needs to more effectively understand, define, and communicate our legal jurisdiction/standing, convey our mission, and exchange data to improve our collaboration with partners, including interagency and international partners, by:

4.7 Including DOI sister agencies (e.g., USFWS) in legislative, regulatory, and policy initiatives.

4.8 Working with states and local entities to improve rapid response/early detection of invasive species, predict new threats through modeling, and develop shared understanding of the definitions of "non-native," "exotic," and "invasive."

4.9 Work outside park boundaries within the confines of available law.

Operations. Workshop participants recommended the following changes to operations:

4.10 Compile, synthesize, analyze, and disseminate existing data about aquatic invasives and affected habitats from sources including the Inventory and Monitoring Networks and Natural Resource Condition Assessments.

4.11 Conduct risk assessments to determine which species will have the most adverse impacts.

4.12 Encourage the NRPC to identify and fund key baseline datasets (inventories) for all ocean and coastal parks to compare impacts of new species.

4.13 Identify scientific gaps and seek new data and researchers.

4.14 Help the NPS expand and better use in-house technical and scientific capacity.

5. Sediment Management and Coastal Infrastructure

Projects related to sediment management, coastal processes, and coastal infrastructure are complex and have ramifications beyond the project timeframe or lifecycle, and can greatly influence the public's perception about federal actions. Protecting cultural resources often means impacts and even impairment of a natural process. The reverse is also true; protection of natural processes (e.g., shoreline migration) has impacts on cultural resources.

Parks lack baseline data and institutional knowledge about natural processes and human impacts on those processes. There is a lack of understanding about potential impacts of park facilities, how to improve the resilience of coastal systems (e.g., habitats, infrastructure) to climate change, how to apply changing storm patterns (e.g., intensities and frequencies), and the impacts resulting from changes in freshwater inputs and throughputs to estuaries and coastal systems. Infrastructure development on non-park lands (inholdings within park boundary and lands outside of park boundary) affects resources in the park. Partnerships with other agencies need to be improved. NPS receives insufficient notification and understanding of projects proposed outside of parks that can impact park resources, processes, or infrastructure.

The existing funding process for sediment management, coastal processes, and coastal infrastructure projects is flawed. Projects that describe an action are funded; projects that propose a study do not compete well for funding. Compliance and impact analysis must be funded prior to decisions about construction or along with construction decisions in a phased approach (i.e., projects should be funded with a compliance phase and a construction phase). Flexible decisions about the most appropriate option for mitigation must be a component of the process. The NPS management policies and guidance should provide better information and examples in several areas (i.e., offshore energy development, beach nourishment, threatened existing infrastructure), but maintain flexibility since parks have different levels of coastal development and varied mandates in their enabling legislation. Parks need additional information about the location of park boundaries and how to adjust them to account for shoreline changes (e.g., erosion, sea level rise).

Director's Order. Workshop participants recommended that the NPS Ocean and Coastal Management Director's Order should include:

5.1   Guidance on offshore renewable energy development, including buffers, off limit areas, minimum acceptable impacts, transmission lines, and use of energy generated within parks, to supplement current NPS Management Policy provisions on utilities and energy management.

5.2   Guidance for the management of offshore cultural resources in light of climate change impacts, such as sea level rise and ocean acidification.

5.3   Guidance (e.g., retreat, relocation, beach nourishment, seawalls, and living shorelines) for responding to sea level rise and coastal changes, and for balancing the impacts on natural and cultural resources.

5.4   Guidance for NPS interaction with other agencies on proposed structures that will have an impact on a park to supplement NPS Management Policies § 4.8.1.1 Shorelines and Barrier Islands.

5.5   Explicit statement that geothermal leasing is not allowed in parks and guidance on the use of geothermal resources by parks to meet internal needs or objectives to supplement NPS Management Policies § 4.8.2.3 Geothermal and Hydrothermal Resources.

5.6   Language that describes the requirements for director approval for utility corridors to supplement NPS Management Policies § 8.6.4.2 Utilities and NPS regulations at 36 C.F.R. § 14.70 through § 14.78.

5.7   Clarification that NPS Management Policy § 9.1.1.5 Siting Facilities to Avoid Natural Hazards applies to existing and threatened facilities and roads, and that the NPS should generally move these facilities, including on barrier islands.

5.8   Clarification on how to meet NPS renewable energy objectives in ocean and coastal parks.

Working Groups. Workshop participants recommended establishing working groups to:

5.9   Develop a decision tree diagram as a method of evaluating when to take action to protect a natural or cultural resource or both (the minimum tool analysis in the wilderness guidelines could be a basis for this tool).

5.10   Recommend revisions to the funding process (e.g., Servicewide Comprehensive Call process for Line Item Construction, NRPP, CRPP, etc.) to ensure that funding for analysis and compliance is specifically granted either prior to or along with a proposed action, such as a construction project, to avoid pre-decisional NEPA analysis.

Operations. Workshop participants recommended the following changes to operations:

5.11   Understand coastal processes at local and regional scales, and manage for resiliency and perpetuation of coastal process-dependent features instead of the current status, population, or issue.

5.12   Incorporate analysis of sustainable infrastructure for historic, non-historic, and archaeological resources in existing planning processes, such as GMPs and RSSs. Insure that park planning scenarios allow for migration of species and habitats (e.g., benthic, water column, beach, dunes).

5.13   Include NRPC and Submerged Resources Center (SRC) resource reviews early in a project's compliance phase, before a project design is initiated.

5.14   Practice adaptive management that allows for iteration between compliance, planning, funding, and implementation. Additional guidance is required on how to develop adaptive management techniques or determine adaptive management objectives.

5.15   Streamline all NPS information management systems (PMIS, FMSS, ASMIS, LCS, and PEPC).

5.16   Modify Servicewide Comprehensive Call to include a fund for immediate projects.

5.17   Encourage cultural resource preparation and management prior to and/or after inundation and emergence.

5.18   Improve administrative records. Use software or other electronic process to file/sort/store electronic documents, such as email and correspondence, so that project knowledge is not lost through staff changes.

Partnerships. Workshop participants recommended that the NPS should strengthen its partnerships and collaboration efforts by:

5.19   Developing relationships with local and regional planners to become more aware of proposed sediment management and coastal infrastructure projects.

5.20   Making the USACE and other agencies aware of NPS mandates and policies early in their planning processes, including NPS permitting requirements.

5.21   Obtaining additional staff to adequately engage with partners.

Appendix A: Workshop Participants

1. Alvear, Elsa: Chief, Resources Management, BISC
2. Anderson, David G.: Fisheries Biologist, REDW
3. Beavers, Rebecca: Coastal Geologist, GRD
4. Beavers, Sallie: Chief of Resource Management, KAHO
5. Bilecki, Michael: Chief, Resource Management, FIIS
6. Boulon, Rafe: Chief, Resources Management, USVI
7. Brunner, Julia: Policy and Regulatory Specialist, GRD
8. Bryant, Richard: Chief, Resources Management, TIMU
9. Cross, Jeffrey: Chief, Ocean and Coastal Resources Branch, WRD
10. Dederich, Peter: Superintendent, SAJH
11. Dickison, George: Director, Natural Resource Program Center
12. DiDonato, Eva: Marine Pollution Ecologist, WRD
13. Echols, Darrell: Deputy Superintendent, CAHA
14. Ellin, Phyllis: Partnerships Liaison, MWRO
15. Eshleman, Jodi: Coastal Engineer, GRD
16. Faulkner, Kate: Chief, Resource Management, CHIS
17. ields, Sherri: Chief, Natural Resources Management, SERO
18. Flora, Mark: Planning and Evaluation Branch Chief, WRD
19. Fradkin, Steve: Chief, Resources Management, OLYM
20. Frost, Bert: Associate Director for Natural Resources Stewardship & Science
21. Glase, Jay: Great Lakes Area Fisheries Biologist, WRD/MWRO
22. Goldsmith, Jay: Assistant Regional Chief Scientist, PWRO
23. Hall, Shelley: Chief, Resources Management, KEFJ
24. Hallac, Dave: Chief, Biological Resources, EVER and DRTO
25. Hamon, Troy: Chief, Resources Management, KATM
26. Hughes, Guy: Chief, Natural Resources Management, KALA
27. Jackson, Bill: Chief, WRD
28. Lepore, Robin: Senior Attorney, DOI Office of the Solicitor
29. Leslie, Elaine: Deputy Division Chief, BRMD
30. Letson, Laura: Ecologist, NOAA (on detail to NPS)
31. Lindsay, James: Chief, Resources Management, PAIS
32. Manski, David: Chief, Resources Management, ACAD
33. Mattix, Carla: Attorney-Advisor, DOI Office of the Solicitor
34. McCoy, Carol: Chief, Planning, Evaluation and Permits Branch, GRD
35. McCreedy, Cliff: Marine Management Specialist, WRD
36. Moraska Lafrancois, Brenda: Aquatic Ecologist, WRD/MWRO
37. Mow, Jeff: Superintendent, KEFJ
38. Neubacher, Don: Superintendent, PORE
39. Pate, Dusty: Natural Resource Manager, JELA
40. Pister, Benjamin: Marine Ecologist & Acting Chief NR and Science, CABR
41. Rice, Bud: Environmental Protection Specialist, AKRO
42. Roman, Charles: North Atlantic Coast CESU
43. Schupp, Courtney: Coastal Geologist, ASIS
44. Seeb, Sami: Archeologist, NPS Submerged Resources Center
45. Smith, Craig: Chief, Resource Management, GLBA
46. Spencer, Page: Chief, Resources Management, LACL
47. Stedeford, Melissa: Planning Project Manager, EQD
48. Steensen, Dave: Chief, GRD
49. Veach, Eric: Chief, Resources Management, WRST

50. Waters, Brenda: Assistant Chief of Natural Resources, INDU
51. Welling, Leigh: Climate Change Response Coordinator, NRSS
52. Williams, Tamara: Hydrologist/Physical Scientist, GOGA
53. Wullschleger, John: Fisheries Biologist, WRD

Workshop Facilitators

1. Bauer, Eva: Computer Specialist, USGS
2. Fisher, Robert: Facilitator, Fisher Collaborative Services LLC
3. Gasser, Jim: Program Analyst, NPS Office of Policy
4. Goodwin, Susan: Conflict Management Specialist, DOI
5. Josupait, Vicky: Outdoor Recreation Planner, BLM
6. Keener, Marcia: Program Analyst, NPS Office of Policy
7. Murdock, Lynne: Interpretive Liaison, NRPC Office of Education & Outreach

Appendix B: Workshop Planning And Agendas

The workshop planning committee consisted of:

- Julia Brunner, Policy/Regulatory Specialist in the Geologic Resources Division;

- Jeffrey Cross, Ocean and Coastal Resources Branch Chief, Water Resources Division;

- Eva DiDonato and Cliff McCreedy of the Ocean and Coastal Resources Branch, Water Resources Division;

- Rebecca Beavers of the Geologic Resources Division;

- Jim Gasser of the NPS Office of Policy;

- Susan Goodwin of the Department of the Interior Office of Collaborative Action and Dispute Resolution; and

- Robert Fisher of Fisher Collaborative Services, LLC.

- Jeff Goehring, a research associate affiliated with the NRPC Office of Education and Outreach, helped the planning committee by developing an Intranet workshop website and populating it with logistical and substantive workshop information and read-ahead materials.

Funding for the workshop was provided by the NRPP servicewide program ($25,000), the Geologic Resources Division ($5,000) and the Water Resources Division ($5,000). These funds were used to:

- hire a professional facilitator, Robert Fisher of Fisher Collaborative Services, LLC;

- provide travel assistance to 27 workshop participants and co-facilitators; and

- provide light refreshments.

Workshop Agenda

Workshop Objectives and Desired Outcomes

- Identify expectations, needs, policies, guidance, and management solutions and tools to effectively manage resources and deal with the priority issues (as identified by participants).

- Develop draft of ocean and coastal management Director's Order and/or other guidance identified as needed by workshop participants.

- Think together strategically and share information and experiences.

- Provide Oceans Program budget update.

- Strengthen NPS oceans/coastal community.

- Enjoy our time together.

Tuesday, August 25th (Millennium Harvest House Hotel Century Room)

11:00-12:00   Gathering
               (please come with a bag lunch if you have not eaten before the noon start time)

| 12:00-12:10 | Welcome |
| | |

Bill Jackson, Chief, Water Resources Division (WRD)
Dave Steensen, Chief, Geologic Resources Division (GRD)

| 12:10-12:25 | Workshop Objectives and Review of Agenda |

Julia Brunner, Policy/Regulatory Specialist, GRD
Jeffrey Cross, Chief, Ocean & Coastal Resources Branch, WRD
Robert Fisher and Susan Goodwin, Facilitators

| 12:25-2:15 | Setting the Stage: Participants Present the Agreed-Upon Priority Issue Areas with Brief Group Discussion |

Objective: Participants will provide an overview of the identified priority issues and share park experiences in dealing with those issues.

Timing: 40 minutes for each priority issue area – presentation (20 minutes) and discussion (20 minutes).

Workshop Priority Issue Areas (determined in advance by participants):
- Climate Change
- Fisheries Management and Impacts of Other Extractive Uses of Resources
- Pollution/Water Quality/Watershed Management
- Aquatic Invasive Species
- Habitat and Ecosystem Restoration
- Coastal Infrastructure/Sediment Management

Content of Participants' Presentations:
- What is the status of this issue area in your park?
- What's worked well and what are the challenges?
- In what ways did you apply the existing NPS Management Policies and legal/regulatory framework? Which provisions were effective? How?
- Are there gaps in the existing NPS Management Policies or the legal/regulatory framework? What is needed to address those gaps?
- What solutions have you accomplished, identified and/or do you suggest for the NPS as a whole to help the NPS better address this issue area?

2:15-2:35	Break
2:35-5:00	Setting the Stage Continued
5:00	Adjourn for the Day
5:30	Get Together at the Millennium Harvest House Hotel Outdoor Gazebo (no-host refreshments)

Wednesday, August 26th (David Skaggs Research Center, NOAA, Room GC-402)

7:30	Shuttle to NOAA starts running.
8:00-8:30	Gathering and Coffee
8:30-8:45	Reflections from Yesterday/Plan for the Day
8:45-10:30	Breakout Sessions by Issue Area: Shaping the Guidance

See detailed Breakout Session Agenda. Also note that each breakout group will discuss its particular issue area in light of improving park resilience to climate change.

10:30-10:50	Break
10:50-12:15	Breakout Sessions -- Continued
12:15-1:00	Lunch
1:00-2:00	Breakout Sessions -- Continued
2:00-3:00	NOAA Demonstration - SOS: Science on a Sphere (meet in 2nd floor lobby)
3:00	Drinks and snacks will be available in the main room.
3:10-4:40	Breakout Sessions -- Continued
4:45-5:00	Full Group Wrap Up (Room GC-402)
5:00	Adjourn for the Day
7:00	Informal working session (note-takers and volunteers) to develop report – presentation (Millennium Harvest House Hotel lobby and other gathering spaces).

Thursday, August 27th (David Skaggs Research Center, NOAA)

7:15	Shuttle to NOAA starts running.
7:30-8:00	Gathering and Coffee
8:00-8:15	Reflections from Yesterday/Plan for the Day (GC-402)
8:15-10:00	Report back from Breakout Sessions

Objective: share two best solutions for each issue area and get/incorporate/provide feedback. Solution can be a draft DO, a recommendation for a legislative proposal, a recommended regulatory revision, recommended content for a fisheries mgmt plan template, etc.

Discussion Questions:
- Do the proposed solutions work for your park/region?
- What are the obstacles and how could they be overcome?
- Are there other solutions too? If so, what are they (please be specific and constructive).

10:00-10:20	Break
10:20-12:15	Breakout Sessions Reconvene/Complete Work on Solutions.
12:15-1:00	Lunch
1:00-2:30	Full Group Review/Summary of Solutions (Room GC-402)

- Presentation and brief discussion (15 minutes for each issue area)
- Themes for the future
- Action items and follow up

2:30-2:50	Break
2:50-4:40	Next Steps

Jeffrey Cross, Julia Brunner and Facilitators

- Oceans Program Update
  - Overview of upcoming opportunities for project funding
  - Brainstorm process options for allocating the funds
  - Next steps
- Issues not fully explored or addressed at the workshop
- Strengthening the NPS Oceans/Coastal Community of Practice
- Action items

4:40-5:00	Closing Remarks
5:00	Adjourn

Breakout Session Agenda

Objectives and Desired Outcomes

- Identify solutions and tools for park units to effectively manage resources and deal with the priority issues.

- Develop draft of ocean and coastal management Director's Order and/or other guidance to implement solutions.

- Discuss the topic in light of improving park resilience to climate change.

- Think together strategically and learn from each other.

Wednesday, August 26th

8:45-8:55	Introductions, review objectives, agenda and roles
8:55-9:30	Discuss expectations – how can we successfully address this topic and improve park resilience to climate change in the future?

9:30-10:30	Identify the range of problems and concerns for this issue area

- Draw on prep materials, issue statements, and information from presentation and discussion yesterday
- Overarching and high-leverage problems
- Brief statement of the problem

10:30-10:50	Break (drinks and snacks available in the main room)
10:50-11:50	Review and revise list of problems and concerns associated with this issue area

- Combine as appropriate, refine the problem definition, additions, etc.

11:50-12:15	Prioritize and select the key problems that will be addressed by the breakout group
12:15-1:00	Lunch
1:00-2:00	Begin working on key problems

For each selected problem:
- Quick review of the existing guidance, policies, practices and legal framework – what's working and what, if anything, needs to change?
- Develop a written statement of the problem
- Determine if the existing framework is considered adequate – if so, determine whether existing description is sufficient or whether to restate
- If the existing framework is considered incomplete or inadequate –
    - Identify and explore a range of potential servicewide solutions to address the problem
    - Agree on the solution
    - Prepare a write-up of the solution – e.g. restatement, proposed guidance language, outline of the ideal NPS approach, list of recommendations, etc.

2:00-3:00	Break for NOAA Demonstration SOS: Science on a Sphere
3:00	Drinks and snacks will be available in the main room
3:10-4:20	Continue working on key problems
4:20-4:40	Prepare brief report for full group tomorrow morning

- Describe problems addressed in detail and problems not addressed yet
- Identify two best solutions to share with the full group – e.g. a draft DO, a recommendation for a legislative proposal, a recommended regulatory revision, recommended content for a mgmt plan template, etc.

4:45-5:00	Full Group Wrap Up (Room GC-402)
5:00	Adjourn for the Day
7:00	Informal working session (note-takers and volunteers) to develop report – presentation (Millennium Harvest House Hotel).

Thursday, August 27th

10:20-12:15   Breakout Sessions Reconvene/Complete Work on Solutions

- Review feedback and common themes
- Complete write-ups of solutions
- Determine what, if anything, to do in the future on any issue not completed or addressed during the Workshop
- Identify any action items and follow up

12:00-12:15   Prepare brief report for full group

12:15-1:00   Lunch

Appendix C: Workshop Proceedings

DAY ONE

The workshop began at 12 p.m. on August 25 in the Millennium Harvest House Hotel with a plenary session for all participants. Opening remarks were provided by Bert Frost, Associate Director for Natural Resources Stewardship and Science; Bill Jackson, Chief, Water Resources Division; Dave Steensen, Chief, Geologic Resources Division; Jeff Cross, Chief, Ocean and Coastal Resources, Water Resources Division; and Julia Brunner, Policy/Regulatory Specialist, Geologic Resources Division. This was followed by three brief, informal presentations by participants on each of the five priority topics. Participants discussed the priority topics and offered potential solutions.

Opening Remarks

The opening speakers welcomed the workshop participants to Boulder. Bert Frost noted the propitious timing of the workshop given the potential budget increase for the WRD Oceans and Coastal Resources Branch, the long lapse of time since the last NPS coastal-related workshop (1999), and the attention that oceans management is currently receiving in Washington.

Bill Jackson observed that the workshop reflected the commitment of park managers and staff to a coordinated, collaborative oceans management effort. This is a significant commitment, given that NPS manages more than 5,100 miles of shoreline. Bill acknowledged the work of Jeff Cross, Julia Brunner, Madonna Baucum, Shannon Kruse, Sybil Winfield, and Jeff Goehring in putting the workshop together. He acknowledged the core NRPC oceans/coastal team including Jeff, Julia, Cliff McCreedy, Rebecca Beavers, Eva DiDonato, and Jodi Eshleman and pointed out that the core team works well across the NRPC, particularly on issues such as aquatic invasives and climate change. Bill noted that workshop participants would be dissecting the high priority issues and developing recommendations, solutions, and a common voice.

Dave Steensen stated that the NPS is poised to undertake major ocean-related tasks and projects, such as the monumental barrier island restoration project proposed at Gulf Islands National Seashore that involves 100 million-year-old sands. Re-examining NPS policies will help establish a common voice, ensure that parks have the necessary tools for addressing these complex issues, and provide servicewide leadership.

Jeff Cross asked the workshop participants to consider climate change in their discussions of all the high priority issues. He requested that the participants identify major threats to biodiversity, and target their recommendations in a way to increase the resiliency of park resources and maintain natural processes.

Julia Brunner requested that the participants review and consider whether the existing NPS Management Policies and guidance are sufficient to help parks address their issues, and if not to develop recommended solutions that are feasible, practical, and helpful to parks. She noted that two attorneys from the Office of the Solicitor were at the workshop to respond to questions, and pointed out that GRD and WRD drafted a handbook explaining NPS jurisdiction principles in ocean and coastal parks. The handbook is under review by attorneys in the Solicitor's Office and the discussions during this workshop will help GRD and WRD refine the handbook.

Robert Fisher pointed out that this workshop is designed to focus on the five issues identified by the participants as their highest priorities. He explained the agenda for the workshop. He also reminded the participants to be complete but brief, to listen attentively, and to look for overlap, disagreements, and different ways of thinking.

Overview of the High Priority Issues
Following the opening remarks, the group discussed the five high priority issues. Each topic was introduced by three of the participants, who briefly described the status of that issue at their park or region, the challenges of managing that issue, any NPS successes, the application of or gaps in NPS Management Policies, and/or recommended solutions. Following the three presentations, the rest of the participants made comments and asked questions.

1. Fisheries Management and Other Extractive Uses
Elsa Alvear, Chief of Resource Management, Biscayne National Park

- Status of this issue area: BISC is 22 miles long and 14 miles wide. The park is mostly marine. It began as a national monument and the park could regulate fishing. It was expanded to a national park and the state regulations apply to fishery management in the expansion areas. The population of South Florida has exploded to 6 million people since the invention of air conditioning in the 1950s. The increased pressure on the park fishery is primarily from recreational fisherman, although there are three commercial shrimping operations with roller-trawls operating in the park. Fishing technology changes, such as fish finders, GPS systems, and larger and more powerful boats, are increasing the pressure on the park's fishery, along with the increased numbers of people.

- Successes and challenges: The statute for the new "expansion area" of the park directs the NPS to regulate fisheries in conformity with state regulations. The park has interpreted this to apply to the entire park and to mean that the state should promulgate fishing regulations for the park. Fish stocks within the park are in worse shape than fish stocks outside the park. Most populations of recreational species are below spawner replacement ratios (e.g., grunts, snappers); 97% of red grouper and 89% of black grouper caught in BISC are below legal size. Some fish in the park are legal-sized, but extremely rare. For example, it took the NPS inventory and monitoring team 600 dives to find one black grouper in the park.

- Suggested solutions: Parks should be held to a higher level of protection than surrounding waters. The formation of a working group of stakeholders and advisors at BISC has been helpful. The park's draft GMP includes five alternatives that are based on desired future conditions. The park's preferred desired future condition is to rebuild and conserve park fisheries resources 20% over current fish size and numbers, with the establishment of marine reserves if necessary. The park requires that fishing violators take a fisheries awareness/education class at the park. This course is offered in English and Spanish and has been highly successful.

Kate Faulkner, Chief of Resource Management, Channel Islands National Park

- Status of this issue: CHIS consists of five islands. The park boundary goes 1 nautical mile offshore. The park is overlain by the NOAA Channel Islands Marine Sanctuary. The state owns the seabed and manages the submerged living resources within the park. The NPS enforces state regulations, and began monitoring kelp beds, fish and invertebrate communities in early 1980s. The park has invested $15 million in monitoring kelp forest, seabirds, and other ocean resources in the park. Many species are over-harvested within the park, including white and black abalone. White abalone was the first marine invertebrate to be listed as an endangered species. The park is missing a keystone predator, the California sea otter.

- Successes and challenges: A network of marine protected areas (MPAs) were established at CHIS in 2003; 21% of waters around the park are now off-limits to fishing. Scientists recommended putting 50% of the park waters into MPAs, but the park ultimately ended up with less than half of that. The establishment of these MPAs took 4-5 years, tens of millions of dollars, the dedication of NPS employees, such as Gary Davis, Dan Richards, and Russ Galipeau, and a good partnership with other entities. The kelp forest monitoring program was doubled in size to provide information about the success of the MPAs. The increases in fish biomass and density and number of species after the first 5 years of MPA status have been documented in a report.

- Application of/gaps in NPS Management Policies: The NPS applies different standards of protection, impairment, and science-based decision-making to marine and terrestrial resources. The NPS Management Policies did not drive the creation of the MPAs at CHIS; there is no language in the Policies about marine resource management (except for sea turtles). Instead, the park applies the general biological provisions of the Policies and enforces state regulations. The state is okay with CHIS regulating some uses (e.g., jet skis).

- Suggested solutions: The NPS should regulate aquatic resources more consistently between fresh and saltwater. The NPS needs baseline and fishery-independent data to rebut the fishing community's argument that there are other reasons for fishery decline than fishing. The data gathered from a small marine reserves established at Anacapa Island in 1978 demonstrated the value of fishery-independent monitoring. The data demonstrated no changes in pollution, water, etc., but increases in fish. The NPS needs to do more outreach by modeling the Pacific Ocean Education Team (POET) efforts and having an ocean Website. The NPS needs a private group, such as fishermen, to champion NPS ocean park protection efforts.

Eric Veach, Chief of Resource Management, Wrangell-St. Elias National Park and Preserve

- Status of this issue: WRST is larger than Switzerland and has higher mountains. It has 125 miles of coastline on the Gulf of Alaska. The harvest of fish is longstanding in the park. The enabling statute allows for some commercial fishing along the coast. WRST has the spawning grounds for Copper River salmon, which transport nutrients into otherwise sterile glacial streams. Now, the harvest of the salmon drives ecosystem processes in the park. Pursuant to the Copper River Salmon Management Plan, 1-1.5 million Copper River salmon are harvested annually; 200,000 go to subsistence fisheries, 50,000 to recreational fishing, and 300,000-500,000 to escapement. Salmon stocks have been declining in the park based on 35 years of data, although some believe that the fishery could be sustainable at current levels.

- Successes and challenges: The NPS Management Policies talk about viability and sustainability, but these levels could be far below park management targets. Management Policies should state why parks are different; NPS should manage for ecosystem processes, not just viable populations. NPS has management authority over Copper River and can open or close the salmon fishery, but has no management authority over the commercial fisheries. The challenge is that the State of Alaska manages resources for maximum sustainable yield. What has worked well is the NPS's ability to regulate the fishery by bringing the State of Alaska and the public to the table.

- Suggested solutions: One solution is to develop a good relationship with the state and with user groups. Another solution is to have a clear vision statement explaining why parks are different from surrounding lands and waters, and why park resources should be managed at the level of ecosystem processes rather than at the level of individual populations.

Fisheries Management Discussion

Comments
- We need more MPAs in park waters. New Zealand has 10% of its coastal areas in protected status. We need to convince commercial fishermen; get them to buy into the concept of MPAs. We can get them to agree individually, but not in groups.

- The State of Hawaii owns the submerged lands at KAHO. NPS rangers cannot enforce state laws on land or in water because of a lack of concurrent jurisdiction, which requires state legislative action.

- At GLBA, the NPS owns the submerged lands, but still has commercial fisheries in the park that are being phased out.

- VIIS would love to reduce fishing, but "customary fishing" is allowed by enabling statute. Groups of fishermen always oppose MPAs, but individually they agree with the concept.

- Areas in Alaska have been closed to commercial fishing by NOAA to protect marine mammals. This concept could be used in parks too.

Questions
- Can MPAs outside of parks have a negative effect on resources, including park fisheries such as GOGA, inside parks? MPAs outside parks could displace fishermen to open areas within parks. Answer: This is a possibility. Parks should have monitoring programs in place to measure those impacts.

- How are MPAs patrolled at Channel Islands? Answer: Park law enforcement (LE) staff is deputized by the State of California. Park LE staff first give warnings to fishing regulation violators, then cite repeat offenders. Fishermen tend to complain that MPAs have no benefit for fish stocks, yet ironically they fish right along the MPA boundary. They also let their gear drift across the boundary. There is not enough enforcement.

- At FIIS, park has jurisdiction over the waters but state has jurisdiction over the benthic resources – can NPS regulate clamming? How can NPS stop the 40-year-old commercial fishery in FIIS, despite the fact that commercial fishing is not allowed in parks unless authorized by law and regulation?

- Is NPS serious in protecting species that are not overfished yet?

Summary of Potential Solutions for Fisheries Management
- Persistent NPS staff/managers.

- Clear explanation why parks need a higher level of protection than surrounding waters.

- Fisheries awareness/education courses.

- Fishery independent monitoring data.

- Public outreach.

- Public/private groups to champion NPS protection efforts.

- Coordinate with user groups.

- More MPAs in park waters.

- Increased law enforcement/citations for fisheries.

2. Pollution, Water Quality, and Watershed Management
Sallie Beavers, Chief of Resource Management, Kaloko-Honokohau National Historical Park

- Status: KAHO was established in 1978 as a result of efforts by a group of Native Hawaiians who sought to have the Honokohau Settlement National Historic Landmark (1962) established as a national park in order to protect it from resort development. The park is about 1200 acres, half of which are land and half are marine. The purpose of the park is to preserve, interpret, and perpetuate traditional Hawaiian culture. Water resources are at the very heart of this culture; the availability of water in the 196 exposed groundwater "anchialine" pools allowed human settlement of the coast. Park water resources are dependent on the Hawaiian water cycle – rain on volcanoes becomes groundwater for drinking; supplies nutrients to reefs, fishponds, and anchialine pools (brackish ecosystems). The quantity and quality of the water resources of the park are in jeopardy from proposed groundwater withdrawals and inputs of nonpoint source pollutants by urban development outside the park. Withdrawals will reduce water quantity and increase the salinity of the exposed groundwater pools. Already the pools have become too brackish to drink. Pollutants travel through the porous lava very quickly and there are no state or county non-point source pollution control measures. This is a natural and cultural resource issue because there is no separation between the two in Hawaiian culture.

- Successes and challenges: What has worked well for the park is obtaining legal standing in administrative proceedings and asking for protective conditions to be placed on developments. If the park is not a legal party in a proceeding that may affect park resources, then the park can only provide public comment. The attorneys in the Solicitor's Office have been extremely helpful. A big challenge is that the park service has not been successful at achieving a regional approach to managing threats from external development. Developments are dealt with one at a time at great cost.

- Application of / gaps in NPS Management Policies: The language in the Policies about external cooperation is helpful but too general. There are gaps in the Policies, which direct parks to take a regional approach and to work with stakeholders. Parks need more specific guidance about avenues that are open to them in working with stakeholders, agencies, and participating in administrative proceedings.

David Manski, Chief of Resource Management, Acadia National Park

- Status: Water quality issues are prevalent in northeastern coastal parks because the area is highly urbanized. Water quality is affected by direct discharge of wastewater treatment plants, such as at Gateway NRA, and also by atmospheric and non-point source pollutants. Much of the non-point source pollutants are found in groundwater, which is hard to monitor and quantify. Most parks in the NPS Northeast Region are collaborating with USGS to ascertain water quality status. Acadia NP is 47,000 acres. The park boundary goes to either mean high or mean low water, depending on the original deed language of the private owners from whose property the park was created. The park includes islands and the mainland and two estuaries. These estuaries are important for recreation and nursery areas for finfish and shellfish, but face eutrophication problems due to the septic systems (that remove pathogens but not nitrogen) of private development that surrounds them.

- Successes and challenges: The challenge is to influence decisions in jurisdictions beyond park boundaries. Acadia NP managers worked with USGS to model effects of land use changes on the local ecosystems. The NPS worked with a local conservation commission and shared this decision support tool. The commission recommended use of the toll and the council adopted it. It's not a perfect model, but it is still being used. The town council sent out a brochure to town residents on how to be good stewards of the estuary.

- Application of / gaps in NPS Management Policies: Many parks in the Northeast Region of the NPS are working with external groups on the nutrient pollution issue, in line with the NPS Management Policies cooperative conservation provisions.

Bud Rice, Environmental Protection Specialist, Alaska Regional Office

- Status: The Alaska coastal parks contain half of the landmass and half of the coastline of the NPS.
- Challenges: These parks are experiencing a variety of pollution-related issues exacerbated by climate change. For example, coastal villages are eroding into the sea due to receding ice and storms where there used to be ice. Indirect effects include increasingly vulnerable oil tanks and a proposed road through a park for relocating the village of Shishmaref. Other pollution issues include cruise ships and ecotourism boats running aground and spilling oil. Another issue is the diminished maintenance of the TransAlaska Pipeline along the Copper River. Alyeska is reducing its staff and closing pump stations thereby reducing its ability to respond to large oil spills. Other issues include mining operations near parks, such as the Red Dog Mine near CAKR and its associated haul road, which puts lead and cadmium dust into the tundra and coastal system. A dredging operation has been proposed along the CAKR shoreline to permit docking of large oil tankers, although there is no funding for this project at this time. Docks along this shoreline impede sediment transport. Other issues include marine debris, and geohazards, such as volcano eruptions that send lahars (mudflows) down rivers, and glacial outburst floods.
- Solutions: Outreach and education are important (e.g., KEFJ and the Alaska Science and Learning Center). NPS programs to reduce greenhouse gas emissions are important. The NPS should continue to work with partners such as NOAA, the state DEC, and the USCG to reduce and respond to spills. The NPS should continue to exert authority and coordinate with regulatory agencies at the Red Dog Mine and get involved in mine development planning (e.g., Pebble Mine, which would be the second largest copper mine in the world). The NPS should participate in geographic response strategy planning —know where resources need to be protected and where equipment is staged in the event of a spill.

Pollution Discussion

Comments
- The NPS coordinator for spill response planning is David L. Anderson, who identifies the highest-priority resources. Geographic response strategies do not constitute an NPS spill response plan. It is advisable to work with other agencies to prepare the geographic response plans, especially for NPS wilderness areas, and to participate in drills with those agencies so that they do make the correct decisions about response on NPS lands.

- Indiana is developing anti-degradation laws for pollution going into Lake Michigan. The challenge is getting the state to understand the vulnerability of park waters and that even a 1% increase in pollution is a big jump.

- Marine debris (including abandoned fishing gear) is a huge issue. FIIS is trying to get involved in international marine debris programs, and BISC has a long history of working with national, international, and park-run marine cleanups. NPS should be on the list of places where volunteers could go to collect marine debris.

- Aquaculture, sunscreen, light, sound, balloons, and emerging contaminants are sources of marine pollution. Oxybenzone in sunscreen affects the recruitment of marine organisms (e.g., may change chemical signature of turtle nesting beaches). NPS should consider advising park visitors to use biodegradable sunscreens. NPS should also work with cruise ship and tourism industries to reduce use of balloons; Florida prohibits the mass release of balloons.

- In general, NPS has more legal and regulatory authority than many employees believe. For example, we can regulate/prohibit marine debris in parks. Below mean high water, parks have authority without regard to the park's level of jurisdiction. NPS could also use other authorities to affect external activities. If there is enough science to document the impacts, the park should work with the Solicitor's Office to develop a regulation or another way to exert NPS interests. Most parks could also adopt a special regulation to put time, place and manner restrictions on fishing.

Summary of Potential Solutions for Pollution

- Obtain legal status to participate in administrative proceedings.

- Decision support tool to model land use changes on the ecosystems for the town planning/council.

- Public outreach and education.

- Working with partners (NOAA, states, USCG) to reduce spills.

- Be involved in geographic response planning.

3. Habitat and Ecosystem Restoration
Dave Hallac, Chief Biological Resources, Everglades and Dry Tortugas National Parks

- Status: Everglades National Park has 1.5 million acres, almost one-third of which is submerged marine/estuarine resources. Florida Bay contains ~400,000 acres and the bottom is designated wilderness. Tom Strickland, the Assistant Secretary of Fish, Wildlife and Parks, recently visited the park and looked through a refractometer and found hypersalinity in the bay due to a lack of freshwater (55 ppt in estuary which should be 10-15 ppt). Just after his visit, a large fish kill was observed. Prolonged hypersalinity may have caused seagrass stress and, in combination with hot water temperatures, caused a seagrass die-off and hypoxic event. The resulted in the largest fish kill ever in the Bay. Multiple stressors caused seagrass to die, which elevated BOD at night and tens of thousands of fish died.

- Challenges: Need to restore Florida Bay so it can deal with natural disturbances and stressors. Restoration projects are difficult because they must balance competing interests, such as the need to get freshwater to the park, for consumptive use, and to prevent flooding of developed areas. Restoration projects are also expensive and direct impacts are better avoided. For example, it would cost billions of dollars for the NPS to restore vessel impacts in EVER. NPS is working on a mitigation bank, based on the wetlands mitigation bank which might be a way for the NPS to obtain funds for restoration. Other challenges include lack of flexibility in the Endangered Species Act.

- Application of / gaps in NPS Management Policies: NPS needs specific Management Policies on management of recreational vessels, such as boats, aiming towards preserving submerged habitats and cultural resources. There are no specific policies for vessel impacts, but that are for personal watercraft and snowmobiles.

- Solutions: The NPS needs to generate specific guidelines for coastal parks to deal with vessel impacts to marine mammals, geologic resources, and submerged aquatic vegetation. The NPS also needs to focus on preventing resource damage; it is much easier to prevent damage than restore it. The NPS should talk to U.S. Fish & Wildlife Service (USFWS) to enhance flexibility in the Endangered Species Act. The NPS also needs to explain to its stakeholders why it needs to build resiliency into its ecosystems before climate change changes everything. Creative solutions that can be used to raise funds for restoration include using mitigation bank to restore wetlands.

David G. Anderson, Fisheries Biologist, Redwoods National & State Parks

- Status: Estuaries are the stepchild of marine management. The Redwood Creek Estuary is partially outside of park boundaries. The estuary/bar-built lagoon in summer is rearing habitat for two threatened salmonid fishes, but also has water quality issues. A 1968 U.S. Army Corps of Engineers (USACE) flood control levee project on the lower 3.4 mi of Redwood Creek cut off the last meander channel, bisected the estuary, and negatively changed circulation and sedimentation patterns and fish habitat. Its effects have been studied for 29 years. The estuary is ready for restoration, but the agencies do not have the funds to initiate it.

- Challenges: Park boundaries do not encompass the entire estuary ecosystem and restoration alternatives will involve adjacent private lands. Another challenge is the difficulty in dealing with USACE limitations to changing Congressionally authorized projects. The project is authorized for funding; the park knows what is wrong with the project and has built relationships with stakeholders, but without a Congressional appropriation to initiate a USACE general investigation study estuary restoration cannot proceed. Nationally, few general investigation studies are funded each year.

- Solutions: The park formed watershed group of local, state, and federal agencies, landowners, and non-profits to work on estuary and levee issues and other watershed problems.. Monitoring and restoration funds are part of the solution to the problem. The park has already conducted public education, biological and geomorphic studies, and made numerous contacts. We need NPS in Washington to champion these restoration issues between the Departments of the Army and Interior and Congress.

Brenda Waters, Assistant Chief of Natural Resources, Indiana Dunes National Lakeshore

- Status: The park consists of 15,000 acres southeast of Chicago, with a boundary 300 feet out in the water and 15 miles of beach along southern Lake Michigan, three miles of which are state park. Lot of visitation to the park, which was created in 1966 and consisted of industrial areas. There has been lots of restoration since then. Projects have focused on prairies, savannas along the shore, and sub-dunal wetlands (Great Marsh-Derby Ditch complex). The park contains two NNLs, and threatened and endangered and fire-dependent species. Park uses prescribed fire for restoration.

- Challenges: Shoreline processes in the park have been very disturbed due to harbors and piers that interrupt littoral drift. Erosion caused by the Michigan City Harbor jetties block littoral drift and necessitates beach nourishment in the park. The park has difficulty working with the USACE. There are also resource impacts from water treatment plants and water intake from the lake. During the development of the White Tail Deer Management Plan, the park was challenged by arguments over jurisdiction with the state and other entities. It is a challenge to restore areas and not get sidetracked following money. Retaining people and funds is also a challenge.

- Application of and gaps in NPS Management Policies: The park uses NPS Management Policies when improving resource conditions, managing natural landscapes, working with partners, doing special designations, and preparing resource management plans and GMPs. The park also relies on its enabling legislation for guidance and partnerships.

- Solutions: Additional staffing and funds are needed for restoration projects, which are generally multi-year (10 years for some projects). One-year soft money does not work. The Great Lakes Restoration Initiative looks like it will fund some longer-term shoreline management and restoration projects.

Habitat and Ecosystem Restoration Discussion
Comments
- The breakout group should consider that not all habitats are as amenable to restoration as others are (e.g., coral reefs are difficult and expensive to restore).

- What are we restoring habitats to? The NPS needs baseline and monitoring data on restoration projects to gauge success/results. We also need to consider shifting baselines and shift our thinking on restoration with climate change.

- We need to get restoration projects to the point where they can maintain themselves. Putting sediment back into the littoral system will help barrier islands become more resilient. Our goals cannot be to recreate what was there in our past.

- Restoration targets using paleo-cores to determine conditions prior to draining Everglades. Fish kill area was <5ppt; now hypersaline. How do we restore to freshwater? NPS doesn't have policies to deal with this problem

- We need to shift our thinking. Climate change will require restoring natural processes or functions, not natural conditions. Management Policies are not explicit about this. We need to ground our manipulations on natural principles. If we manipulate things that haven't happened before, we could be pushed to do things that aren't natural.

- Mississippi Coastal Improvement Program (MiCIP) is a successful application of the NPS Management Policies. The NPS relied on Section 4.8.1.1 for two reasons. First, this section allows parks to restore areas that have been impacted by anthropogenic activities or structures. In this case, USGS published papers contending that the Mississippi barrier islands in Gulf Islands National Seashore have been impacted by years of dredging and offshore sediment disposal (of 22 million cubic yards). Some level of restoration of these islands would be consistent with the NPS policies. Second, the NPS relied on this section to explain to the State of Mississippi and the USACE why the NPS would not agree to 10-foot high dunes on the fill between East and West Ship Island; 10-foot dunes never occurred there naturally.

- MiCIP will dump 22 Mcu yd of sediment offshore. The GUIS islands will not go back to state in late 1800s; face sea level rise, storms, etc. Should we put more sediment back into system to be more resilient? How do we do that without creating more damage? Need to look at restoring processes, not what we had in the past. Do our policies support that?

- NPS does not have policies to help with other ocean/coastal issues, such as resolving the balance between natural and cultural resources.

- NPS needs to draft legislation to broaden our authority over ocean/coastal resources (e.g., Thomas bill). Congress could reaffirm stronger authority on areas within our boundaries.

- DOI is working on national partnership agreement with USACE.

Summary of Potential Solutions for Restoration

- NPS needs to explain why it needs to build resiliency into ecosystems as an effective response to climate change.

- NPS restoration policies should focus on natural processes/functions, rather than restoring to historic natural conditions.

- Restorations/manipulations need to be based on scientific principles.

4. Aquatic Invasive Species
Jay Goldsmith, Assistant Chief Regional Scientist, Pacific West Region

- Status: San Francisco Bay, which includes Golden Gate National Recreation Area, has 250 invasive species, the most invasive species of any estuary in North America. American Samoa National Park has few problems with invasive species. NPS does not have good information about aquatic invasives; we have not monitored them as well as terrestrial invasives.

- Challenges: We do not have a full understanding of the scope of the problem because it is difficult to see and monitor the invasives underwater.

- Application of/gaps in existing NPS Management Policies: Section 4.4.4 has proved to be a good policy and Section 4.4.2 (removal) provides some guidance. But Golden Gate needs additional resources more than management policies. More guidance won't solve the problems. Golden Gate probably cannot eradicate or control invasive species because they are well established. Parks need strategies to prioritize species for action; other species might have no control strategies. There is no model strategy and one should be developed. For example, the State of California has an aquatic invasive species management plan with 163 action items (not approved or funded yet).

- Solutions: NPS understands what to do with aquatic invasives; key issues are collaboration and coordination. Parks need prevention, long-term control and management, education/outreach, research, laws and regulation. Parks need staffing, expertise, and funding at the park level to make progress; more guidance won't solve the problem. Probably cannot eradicate or control all invasives. Monitoring needs to address multiple species and their changing interaction, roles, and synergies. Since invasive species adapt well, they will adapt to climate change. Some species that are not much problem now may become big problems; synergies between benign species and another invasive that makes benign species more problematic.

Brenda Moraska Lafrancois, Aquatic Ecologist, Mid-West Region

- Status: The Great Lakes are connected to oceans via St. Lawrence Seaway to the Atlantic Ocean, the Illinois River to Gulf of Mexico, and through Canada to the Hudson Bay. These Great Lakes parks have substantial resources and 182 documented invasive species (including: sea lamprey, alewife, quagga and zebra mussels, gobies, and zooplankton), most of which arrived after the opening of the St. Lawrence Seaway in the 1950s. The sea lamprey was introduced in late 19th century and devastated commercial fisheries. Alewife and rainbow smelt have been commercial fisheries and pest species. On average, one new species arrives every six months and 65% of the species arrived via ballast water releases. Species also arrive via accidental releases, bait and aquarium releases, and aquaculture. Some species are intentionally introduced, such as Pacific salmon that was introduced and promoted by the state (which has different objectives than NPS). The lower Great Lakes benthic systems are mostly on non-native species. Lake Superior has been somewhat protected from aquatic invasive species because of the cold water.

- Challenges: Identifying the vectors of species is complicated; they range from individual anglers to large industries. There are problems navigating jurisdictional issues with various entities with authorities (e.g., ballast water overseen by several agencies). Climate change – cold waters have protected Lake Superior; warmer waters may enable invasive species to survive. NPS needs baseline data on biological communities in nearshore waters to determine impacts of new species. The baseline is shifting with climate change. We also need risk assessments to determine which species will have the most adverse impacts. Need to work with states and other agencies to change management activities that maintain status quo or sustain certain invasives (such as alewife and smelt mentioned above).

- Solutions: The best solution is prevention and coordination with agencies. No established aquatic invasive species has been eradicated. We need to stay involved in legislative/policy initiatives, make helpful legislative changes (i.e., in key vectors like ballast water), and do education campaigns, such as "Stop Aquatic Hitchhikers" and "Habitatitude," which have been successful.

Page Spencer, Chief of Resources Management, Lake Clark National Park & Preserve

- Status: There is more coastline in Alaska than all of the lower 48 states. There are few documented invasive species, mostly because there are not many people looking for them. Cold water and distant location protected Alaska, but the climate is becoming warmer and LACL is closer to the rest of the world. The threats: 1) Atlantic salmon escaping from farm pens in British Columbia; bring disease; stray into wild rivers. 2) Rats come on ships; have been on the islands for over 200 years. They are eradicating ground-nesting seabirds because of no predators. USFWS starting eradication program in Aleutians. 3) Vectors spread invasives; ballast water; ship wrecks; boots on anglers (felt soles to be outlawed); float planes from Lake Hood.

- Successes and challenges: The rat eradication program has been pretty successful, but it is also very expensive and has bycatch problems. A challenge is that lots of ships from Asia are traveling to the lower 48 and bringing invasive species. Other vectors include: ballast water, shipwrecks, felt-soled waders (about to be outlawed in AK), and seaplanes.

- Solutions: Our paperwork exercise needs to include other countries and state agencies; stop being so insular. We need to include federal, state agencies, and other countries in resource protection. We need to wash our feet, boats and floats. We need more resources.

Aquatic Invasive Species Discussion

Comments
- The zebra-quagga mussel plan that was put together by BRMD and WRD is a good resource. Good tools for viral hemorragic septicemea (VHS).

- With climate change, what is an invasive species? Should the definition of invasives include species whose range is changing (e.g., riparian species such as Phragmites and loosestrife)?

- We need to keep pushing for NPS to be included in the USCG rulemaking process for ballast water.

- A good reference manual on aquatic nuisance species (ANS) was started last fall.

- Spill response actions can bring in lots of invasives like rats in batting used to clean up oil. USCG now storing materials for CHIS separately to avoid contaminating islands with rats in the event of a spill.

- Think about regulations and carrot and sticks. For example, washing boats and gear in lakes without mussels may cause fishermen to illegally introduce them in order to avoid having to comply with such requirements.

- Cruise ships in GLBA – concession permit doesn't allow them to discharge ballast water or foul water in bay.

- NPS needs to get to the media to emphasize ecological impacts, not just financial impact of invasives on water intake lines and other infrastructure impacts. How do we change that?

- Part of the solution is education and getting non-resource people to help with the message. CABR gets 100,000 visitors to the intertidal each year, but there are no programs for visitors there.

- EVER tried to use python as poster child to highlight invasive species problems through education, but it's not getting much traction. Act with USFWS more (Lacy Act). Think about impacts of invasive species on ecosystem services.

- NPS need to tighten down on laws, and work with DOI and other regulatory agencies. For example, concession permits in GLBA prohibit ballast water discharge in parks

- The ANS breakout group needs to think about disease, endocrine disrupters, and emerging wildlife disease.

- How do we use the synergies/overlap between fisheries and invasive species groups?

- Impacts of invasives on submerged cultural resources. Collaborate with SRC; it can help with detection, outreach and education with natural resources.

- Marine invasives such as lionfish could impair reefs in FL, Caribbean, Pacific reefs.

Summary of Potential Solutions for Invasives
- Prevention.

- Baseline data on biological communities in nearshore waters to compare impacts of new species.

- Risk assessments to determine which species will have the most adverse impacts.

- Involvement in legislative and policy initiatives.

- Education and getting non-resource people in NPS to help with the message.

5. Sediment Management and Coastal Infrastructure
Michael Bilecki, Chief of Resource Management, Fire Island National Seashore

- Status: There are 92 parks in the Northeast Region and 10 are ocean and coastal parks; most have sediment management issues. At Sagamore Hill NHS, an adjacent landowner dredges right next to park and dumps it elsewhere without a permit creating a water quality issue. The park's challenge is working with state DEC. At George Washington Birthplace there's erosion along the Potomac, but they may have a solution –unblock the creeks. At Gateway NRA, Sandy Hook and Jamaica Bay have sediment issues. At Sandy Hook, the access road has washed away a couple times and was rebuilt; beach nourishment projects pump sand from offshore onto the ocean beaches and need to continue. Jamaica Bay is losing wetlands and the park is researching whether dredge material can be used to build up elevation with sea level rise. At Assateague Island NS, the jetties of resort community of Ocean City just north of the park have blocked sand flowing north to south coupled with washovers result in loss of piping plover habitat. ASIS is working with USACE on bypass process; where will the money and sediment come from? Within FIIS, there are 17 communities and 4,200 homes; 200 homes are built on primary dunes. There are also bayside homes with bulkheads to counter the erosion caused by subsidence and sea level rise. 15 million people reside within 60 miles of the park. 13 ferry north-south channels come into the park interrupt bayside sediment transport. The park took over a bayside marina that causes erosion in park's Sunken Forest. The park contains a federally designated wilderness (7 miles out of the 26 shoreline miles). FIIS has three issues: 1) counties and communities want beach nourishment; take sand offshore and pump in on beaches. 2) USACE working on a long-term (40 yrs) storm damage protection plan (the Fire Island to Montauk Point plan) to protect Long Island, which proposes beach nourishment along the FIIS shoreline. FIIS enabling statute requires that erosion control or shoreline protection measures take place in accordance with a plan that is mutually acceptable to DOI and Dept of the Army; they haven't agreed in 30 yrs. 3) Erosion of marsh elevation (erosion and subsidence).

31

200 homes on bayside have bulkheads; areas not bulkheaded erode; ferry channels move sand to wrong areas.

- Success and Challenges: The beach nourishment project at ASIS is a success. A big challenge is getting money for projects; another is a lack of data; another is that dredging sand from offshore and using it for community beach nourishment projects reduces sand supply to the parks for natural replenishment. FIIS worked with communities contributed to success. The park is working with the state on a dredged material management plan, but that plan won't be completed before dredging happens. The park received $250K for stabilization project that involves dredging sand from a channel. The park needs a state permit to put sand on state bottomlands.

- Application of/ gaps in NPS Management Policies: FIIS got a policy waiver to write FONSI for EAs for the last two beach nourishment projects. In future, projects will need an EIS. Do our policies work? Yes.

Tamara Williams, Hydrologist, Golden Gate National Recreation Area

- Status: Golden Gate NRA extends a quarter-mile offshore, along 40 miles of the San Francisco Bay shore and outer coastline. San Francisco Bay is outflow for 40% of state waters; the park also includes other smaller coastal watersheds.. There is no sediment management plan for San Francisco Bay. One issue is placement of dredge materials within and outside the bay. Not enough information about sediment processes in the bay. Infrastructure near parklands includes the Great Highway along Ocean Beach in San Francisco, marinas, Highway 1, wastewater outfalls, etc. There are many historic military facilities along the coastline, such as World War II batteries on the bluffs, some of which have fallen onto the beach below.

- Successes and challenges: GOGA is at the table with other agencies, land managers, municipalities, etc. working to find common ground. The park understands effects of sea walls and other coastal structures on adjacent neighbors and NPS dunes. Challenges include lack of understanding of sediment management, specifically what it takes to maintain beaches and roadways. Another challenge is not being at the table with other planning and management entities. The park needs enough NPS staff to keep NPS interests at the forefront and we need the data, understanding, and a common vocabulary. There is no sediment management plan for San Francisco Bay. Such a plan is needed to address issues such as nourishment of beaches, dredging and placement of materials, sand mining, and the management of the sewer system under the Great Highway immediately landward of Ocean Beach.

- Solutions: NPS needs to work with the USGS, the USACE, the Bay Conservation and Development Commission, the Marine Sanctuaries, and other management agencies within the region. We must understand and restore natural processes.

Shelley Hall, Chief of Resources, Kenai Fjords National Park

- Status: KEFJ doesn't have anthropogenic impacts on sediment; it does have lots of natural sediment issues and natural phenomena, such as glaciers, volcanoes, lahars, and earthquakes that at affect natural resources (e.g., species tied to glaciers and glacial silt); the park can't do much about them. Natural erosion causing some issues with cultural resources – lodge built on lagoon in KEFJ, sensitive habitat from which visitors can travel on ATVs to coastal meadows to see bears. Elsewhere in Alaska, the presence of the Red Dog Mine has caused sediment issues on the coast. Cultural resources can be affected by natural sediment movement, such as at Klondike Gold Rush and Katmai.

- Successes and challenges: The most challenging issue in Alaska coastal parks is understanding jurisdiction because of Mean High Water. Other jurisdiction issues revolve around native corporation inholdings; ANILCA allows native corporations to own lands, subsurface rights, and cultural resources. All islands offshore belong to the USFWS. As glaciers recede, exposed islands go from NPS jurisdiction to USFWS jurisdiction.

- Solutions: Partnerships; parks can't handle the issues alone.

Sediment Management and Coastal Infrastructure Discussion

Comments
- Current NPS guidance on sediment is very limited; policies say almost nothing. NPS needs more guidance. Armoring is taking place to protect cultural resources; shoreline armoring will affect wetlands. NPS has EO and other guidance about wetland impacts.

- Coastal infrastructure and sediment management are complicated issues and our policies don't say much about them, especially shoreline armoring.

- Coastal infrastructure includes offshore energy, transmission lines across the park (right-of-way to access the grid for energy development), and roads. Coastal infrastructure related to offshore wind energy will pose problems to parks. These need to be addressed by NPS.

- NPS needs clarity on how and where to replace storm-damaged infrastructure. Parks in the Southeast Region are prone to hurricanes that damage and destroy roads, buildings, and lighthouses. There is talk about moving buildings to more stable places. Roads are often replaced in their previous locations.

- Mapping benthic habitats is key. We also need habitat baseline information and reservoir inundation studies to learn what happens to cultural sites when they go under water. Once cultural sites are underwater they are still managed. Submerged Resources Center has remote sensing equipment that could help with mapping.

- Boundaries of some parks today will change with erosion. CAHA has migrated outside its boundary. The beach is now outside of the park and park boundary is now in the water. Park lost a beach to erosion over 10 years; management has to change. Infrastructure can pit natural and cultural resource issues against each other; managers will make decisions.

- There is good sediment and bad sediment. Sedimentation is a natural process but sometimes is altered by human activities and structures.

- Defining USACE responsibilities for the environment. There are 950 USACE employees in Jacksonville, FL. What are the opportunities? How can the NPS and USACE enhance cooperation?

- Guidance on what triggers legal action would be helpful. What is serious enough to trigger that action?

Questions
- Which breakout group should tackle watershed management/sediment links? Deforestation (cutting, fires) in island watersheds and feral animals increase erosion downstream; sediments cover coral reefs.

- What is true scope of Federal Advisory Committee Act prohibitions? Could we do fast-track charters?

- How can we work better with other bureaus/agencies whose missions conflict with ours?

- Lots of talk about partnerships; are policies in place to support them? Economy Act is only thing we have to support partnerships. FACA restricts ability to work with other partners. FACA doesn't restrict parks from meeting with outside groups individually. NPS can't bring all the factions together to hash out recommendation and then act on that advice

Summary of Potential Solutions for Sediment Management and Coastal Infrastructure
- Work more with other agencies and partners.

- Develop list of authorities and guidance for spending money beyond park boundaries.

- We need to get more info about FACA out to parks.

DAY TWO

Problem Identification

On August 26 and 27, the workshop participants moved to the National Oceanic and Atmospheric Administration (NOAA) David Skaggs Research Center. Participants divided into five breakout groups. Each group addressed one of the priority topics by describing and prioritizing the problems associated with that topic and identifying potential solutions. Each breakout group was led by a facilitator, and the discussions and recommendations were captured by note-takers.

1. Fisheries Management and Other Extractive Uses

The fisheries management breakout group agreed that submerged ocean and coastal park natural resources are not managed in the same way as terrestrial resources and parks need guidance, standards, and strategies to achieve management of submerged natural resources consistent with NPS goals. Cooperation with management partners (i.e., states and fishery management councils) is essential because fish populations extend beyond park boundaries. Parks and fishery management agencies do not always have the same mission and goals (protection vs. harvest), and state agencies focus on stocks levels rather than park fishery resources, so it can be difficult for NPS to get a "seat at the table." Some parks do not understand their jurisdiction and authorities, and existing fishery regulations (e.g., bag and size limits, seasons, illegal harvest) are not always enforced (low priority and shortage of law enforcement rangers). It is not clear if NPS is managing for a "snapshot in time" or trying to preserve ecosystem function. In the face of climate change, more aggressive management actions (e.g., assisted migration, genetic manipulation for species more adaptable to climate change) may be necessary. Servicewide guidance and tools are needed to manage fish and ecosystems to increase resiliency.

Problem Statement on Ecosystem Management: Current management focuses on stocks, populations, and individual species, not on ecosystems. Legal and illegal harvesting has resulted in population declines that affect ecosystem integrity and resilience to climate change. The indirect effects of fishing (e.g., incidental or by-catch, habitat destruction, derelict fishing gear, lights, etc.) adversely impact NPS resources, ecosystems, and ecosystem services. Influences beyond park boundaries (e.g., energy development, mariculture, fish stocking, etc.) have the potential to adversely impact NPS resources, ecosystems, and ecosystem services. The effects of climate change will exacerbate adverse impacts on NPS resources and create further stress on ecosystem functions.

Solutions

Short-term

- Implement 2009 NPS-NOAA MOU; explore other interagency agreements for data sharing

- Create an NPS working group to develop ecosystem management language appropriate for a DO (list of principles that reflect management for resiliency (e.g., do this, not this); manage for optimum sustainable yield (OSY) not maximum sustainable yield (MSY); removing nonnative species, repatriating extirpated species, etc.) for DO language to begin the paradigm shift

  - Define NPS management objectives for fishing management (8.2.5.5)

  - Principles

  - Regional approaches

  - Directives

  - 4.4.1.2 and 4.4.3 – too general

- Identify a state or region to test ecosystem-based management

- Create formal coastal networks for coordination, etc. (e.g., Colorado River Board, Alaska parks)

- Participate with NOAA MPA Center to nominate ocean and coastal parks to national list (10 already listed; 30 to be nominated in fall 2009) and in MPA gap/threat analyses.

- Implement and monitor no-take areas in each unit/pilot project to have a natural standard/control with an undisturbed population for comparison and restoration

- Gather data on species that may not be overfished; create special regulations to protect them (4.4.2.1. and 4.4.3 too general)

- Funding mechanisms need to support ecosystem management/climate change; PMIS supports crisis management, not proactive projects

- Develop park- or MPA-specific Fisheries Management Plans

- Increased surveys and monitoring of fish populations

- Increased management of marine debris in important habitat (e.g. coral reefs)

- Increased number of law enforcement officers dedicated to fisheries resources

Mid-long-term

- Develop management directives that initiate the paradigm shift to ecosystem management in the field

- Develop regional approaches to implement ecosystem management among parks (4.4.2)

  - Establish formal coastal networks (e.g., CABR, CHIS, GOGA, PORE; GLBA, WRST, KLON, etc.). (Colorado River Board model)

  - Conduct case study of park-federal agencies-state (CHIS, FL, Lake Superior parks)

- Recognize, support, and work with partners, including ecosystem management and climate change science

- Develop national policy to implement and monitor no-take areas in each unit; determine what the unexploited populations, habitats, ecosystems look like as baseline to measure impacts/undisturbed natural standard

- Plan networks of MPAs, with NPS collaborating with other federal and state agencies.
- Manage within boundary to maintain or increase, as appropriate, biodiversity and natural processes
- Increase ecosystem resiliency to address impacts of climate change and increase options for adaptation by:
    - Restoration and seed projects (e.g. Great Lakes, water management, restore coastal and fluvial processes)
    - Protecting species not over-fished yet (e.g. rockfish species, grunts)
    - Manage for healthy fish populations rather than MSY
    - Define viable fish populations
    - Participate in regional fishery decisions
    - Define and describe the seamless networks for active participation
- Identify and monitor key indicators to measure success (e.g. presence of high-level predators, healthy fish populations, biodiversity, etc.)
- Collect data to support science-based ecosystem management (e.g. habitat, physical oceanography, telemetry, etc.)
- Incorporate ecosystem goals into resource management plans and resource stewardship strategies
- Create fisheries management plans (stewardship, allocation)
- Clarify scale of ecosystem-based management – what can be done at the park level and at the regional level if they don't approximate the boundaries of the ecosystem
- Develop cooperating agreements with states to encourage ecosystem-based management

Problem Statement on Double Standard for Aquatic and Terrestrial Resources: NPS allows activities within ocean and coastal parks, such as harvest and enhancement that are not allowed in terrestrial systems. Recreational and traditional fishing are allowed, unless prohibited by enabling legislation; recreational hunting is typically not allowed. Protect and preserve are applied to terrestrial systems, not to aquatic and marine systems.

Solutions
Eliminate double standard. Elevate management of aquatic and marine systems to be comparable with management of terrestrial systems to ensure ecosystem integrity.
- Recreational fishing is not prohibited – the goal is to rebuild over exploited populations to increase resiliency to climate change. All tools will be considered, including harvest restrictions and no-take areas.
- Clarify competing objectives – harvest vs. protection; make no fishing the default to get parity between hunting and fishing.

Problem Statement on Managing for Ecosystem Function/Processes vs. Snapshot in Time: The original NPS paradigm and current management philosophy is based on pre-settlement America and the static condition of park resources. Is NPS managing a museum or an ecosystem? Parks have already experienced changes due to broader ecosystem modifications as a result of climate change and the introduction of new species. Climate change will result in changes in the distribution and abundance of species and new assemblages and relationships. Parks need guidance on how to respond.

Solutions

Provide guidance to change the paradigm from managing static locations and single species to managing dynamic ecosystems.

- Identify and manage stressors and human factors, while leaving natural systems predominant over human uses.

- Manage so that natural processes predominate over human effects, other than climate change.

- Deal with uncertainty and the inability to halt changes to species, habitats and communities in parks.

- Manage wild areas, regardless of changes

- Minimize human intervention, influence, and impacts

- Maintain processes with least human intervention to manage the processes

- Protect and manage fisheries to increase resiliency of ecosystem functions and processes

Problem Statement on Jurisdiction and Ownership: The terms exclusive, concurrent, proprietary, bottom-lands, and submerged lands are often confusing to parks. The applicability of 36 CFR 2.3 to proprietary jurisdiction is confusing. Parks often do not know the extent of their marine boundaries and sea level rise will affect boundaries. How do parks manage species with life cycles that occur outside park boundaries? Parks and stakeholders do not understand, or disagree on, jurisdiction, legal authority, and treaty rights.

Solutions

Short-term

- Parks need clear understanding of jurisdiction, legal authority, and treaty rights and communicate that to stakeholders

- Parks need to know difference between ownership and jurisdiction

- Clear guidance on issues of scale in ecosystem-based management – parks are local and regional; a lot is beyond NPS control

- Guidance on external impacts management (e.g., energy, aquaculture, marine debris, etc.)

- Policies to support park when it is the decision-maker and when it is not the decision-maker

- Clarify enabling legislation – primary resource occurs outside park boundaries leads to conflicts about competing objectives (harvest vs. protection)

- Publish jurisdiction handbook; communicate with the parks (staffs, LEs, etc.)

- Use Webinars to share best practices and learning

- In the absence of clear legal authority or agreement on jurisdiction, temporarily seek common ground with states and others to pursue better stewardship of fisheries – state as a cooperating agency

Mid-long-term

- Park-by-park analysis of jurisdiction, authorities, and boundaries

- Develop legislative language to affect management of resources beyond park boundaries

- Collaborate with partners and explore options for expanding jurisdiction over species that spend part of their lifecycles outside park boundaries

- Legislative changes to park boundaries

2. Pollution, Water Quality, and Watershed Management

The waters and associated resources of National Parks are threatened by internal and external sources of pollution. Solutions to water quality problems differ depending on the source. Existing laws and state and federal programs have not been effective in protecting water quality in the National Parks. Traditionally, the NPS has focused on water quality within park boundaries, which has limited the ability of parks to manage water quality issues. There is a clear need to focus outside park boundaries to effectively protect park resources. NPS managers often lack the information to effectively manage coastal water resources and they need guidance on authorities and jurisdiction related to coastal water resources. Nutrient enrichment and contaminants are priority issues. Other issues discussed include: pathogens, altered salinity, light and sound pollution, marine debris, water clarity, and ocean acidification.

Problem Statement on Nutrients, Contaminants, and Pathogens from External Sources: Pollution of NPS ocean and coastal waters arrives from various sources via multiple pathways external to parks and causes a variety of impacts within parks, including algal blooms, hypoxic conditions, fish kills, and change in the structure and function of ecosystems, all of which can degrade visitor experience. Parks need to identify and monitor pollution impacts on coastal resources. They need to develop effective prevention and response strategies to human-caused pollution and effects of climate change and their interactions. The USEPA regulatory process is not responsive to NPS needs because the criteria for Tier III waters do not recognize parks as federally protected resource areas. Parks must demonstrate that their waters are pristine to be designated as protected waters. NPS Management Policies in chapters 3 and 4 are not strong enough to deal with water quality through Cooperative Conservation and Partnerships.

Solutions
Improve and participate more effectively in the state and federal water quality regulatory processes.

- Develop a DOI-USEPA MOA at national and regional levels to protect and enhance DOI resource area waters.

- Work with USEPA to revise USEPA regulations and guidance documents to improve the process of Tier III water designation and USEPA Regional Office oversight of state permits affecting parks.

  - Accelerate the pace of state designation of Tier III waters through USEPA's grant, schedules, oversight processes.

  - Develop water quality standards for nitrogen, phosphorous, and emerging contaminants and, under the Clean Air Act, develop air emissions standards for mercury.

  - Require notice of NPDES permit actions to all park units/affiliated areas within the watershed/aquifer.

  - Create federal agency appeal process for NPDES permits to USEPA Regional Office of state delegated permits before permit is finalized.

  - Improve the state NPDES permit review process to address alternatives so permits focus on impacts to ecological systems and include better treatment options.

- Tighten Clean Water Act anti-degradation regulations for parks and non-point source programs through USEPA, the Coastal Zone Reauthorization Act, and state non-point source programs, including increasing regulatory mechanisms.

- Identify impaired waters that negatively affect coastal park water quality. Participate in the TMDL process to bring listed waters into compliance with Clean Water Act standards.

Create guidance explaining how to work through the federal regulatory system in order to obtain the highest protection for park waters.

- Provide park managers with information and guidance on how to use existing tools, such as obtaining legal status to intervene in local jurisdiction permit decisions. Request that conditions such as BMPs are placed on developers.

- Assemble tools/examples for increasing awareness of park resources and regulatory issues by local and state agencies. One example is the decision support tool developed at Acadia National Park to model land use changes on the ecosystems for the town planning/council.

- Provide internal NPS/DOI technical assistance to park managers regarding appropriate conditions and best management practices.

- Compile a library of exhibits/examples of adverse impacts in parks from pollution. This would be helpful to NPS in presenting arguments to permit authorities when developments may impact park resources.

- Provide a synopsis of authorities and guidance that enable NPS to address problems originating outside park boundaries.

- Actively participate in a regional approach (local/watershed/aquifer) to cooperatively manage local and park water resources.

- Use partnerships to identify important land parcels to protect through conservation easements or acquisition.

Problem Statement on Nutrients, Contaminants and Pathogens from Internal Sources: Pollution of NPS ocean and coastal waters from internal sources can lead to multiple impacts within parks, such as algal blooms, hypoxic conditions, fish kills, and change ecosystem structure and function, all of which can degrade visitor experience. Control of internal pollution sources requires attention to facilities, for example, septic systems, marinas, roads and parking lots and fuel tanks, as well as attention to activities and operations such as, agricultural leases, concessions, landscaping practices, and pesticide use. NPS Management Policies in chapters 1 and 9 discuss sustainability of park facilities, activities and operations, but the language is insufficient to protect water quality in our coastal parks.

Solutions
- Require all new park infrastructure to use best available technologies and practices to protect park waters from input of nutrients, contaminants, and pathogens.

- Require the planning, compliance, and siting of new facilities to consider sea level rise and other coastal climate change issues.

- Require all parks to assess facilities that have the potential to adversely affect coastal water resources. These projects should be high priority for funding.

- Require known facilities that are significantly degrading water quality be given funding priority to upgrade to best available technologies. All NPS funding sources should weigh funding criteria to favor correcting these failed systems.

- Require that over the near term (20 years) all facilities will be replaced with best available technologies to protect park waters from input of nutrients, contaminants, and pathogens.

- Showcase to visitors, agencies, and community groups the best management practices that parks use to protect coastal water quality.

- To begin to accomplish these efforts, we recommend forming a working group consisting of maintenance and natural and cultural resource staffs from parks.

3. Habitat and Ecosystem Restoration

Coastal and marine habitats and biodiversity in parks are under increasing threats and stress from habitat fragmentation and degradation due to development, watershed alteration, water withdrawal and pollution, and consumptive uses of land and water resources. Parks are not able to effectively restore ecosystems to achieve their mandate to conserve parks unimpaired for the enjoyment of current and future generations. Climate change and other stressors are causing the NPS to rethink habitat restoration in light of abrupt and ongoing impacts from sea level rise, lake level change, ocean warming, ocean acidification, storms, and other phenomena. The NPS must pursue adaptation and restoration strategies that ensure ecological integrity and resilience of park resources. The NPS should focus on restoring natural processes to restore resilience.

The restoration breakout group identified the following problems and issues:

- Lack of baseline or reference condition as a restoration goal. Restoration effort should restore natural processes (i.e., watershed integrity, hydrologic characteristics, plant and animal community composition, etc.). The definition of natural condition for restoring disturbed areas under the current management policies is too vague.

- Lack of applied research and monitoring deters adaptive management and inhibits learning and evaluation of restoration results.

- Inconsistent project development servicewide and inadequate funding for coastal restoration (NRPP funding is insufficient and line-item construction funding priorities do not favor habitat restoration).

- Habitat protection is more effective and much less costly than restoring damage after the fact. Policies and guidance should emphasize prevention of vessel groundings, avoiding alteration of natural processes, avoiding release of invasive species, and early detection of invasions.

- Many factors or threats affecting park resources emanate from outside of park boundaries and NPS jurisdiction.

- State or federal agencies, such as USACE, often have missions that are different from or contradict the mandates of the NPS.

- Single species focus on T&E recovery may conflict with habitat or ecological restoration goals.

- Extirpated species restoration may cause community concerns and internal conflicts with visitor use and park management.

- NEPA compliance may not be relevant to changing conditions and time and cost constraints may exceed budgets and timelines.

- NPS does not plan or manage resources at landscape and bioregional levels.

Problem Statement on Inconsistent Servicewide Approach to Ecological Restoration for Coastal and Marine Habitats: All the factors above hinder NPS in successfully addressing restoration across coastal and marine resources in the National Park System. NPS efforts should restore natural processes and characteristics of healthy, fully functioning ecosystems. NPS does not plan or manage resources at landscape and bioregional scales, which is critical for the agency to address the impacts of climate change, to address factors or threats emanating from outside park boundaries and NPS jurisdiction, and to work with federal and state partners at the bioregional level. Establishing baseline or reference conditions including the current definition of natural conditions for restoring disturbed areas under the current management policies should be reviewed. Lack of applied research and monitoring deters adaptive management and inhibits learning and evaluation of restoration results. Finally, NEPA compliance may not be relevant to changing conditions and time and cost constraints may exceed budgets and timelines.

Solutions
- Organize a working group to draft guidance to direct coastal and marine habitat and ecosystem restoration to restore natural processes and resilience at the park, landscape, and bioregional levels (i.e., watershed integrity, hydrologic characteristics, plant and animal community composition, establishing marine reserves, etc.).

- The policy should include Research Natural Areas (i.e., no-take marine reserves) for restoring and maintaining natural processes and communities and for comparative analysis with outside areas.

- Coastal and lacustrine wetland restoration goals and objectives need to be defined because no net-loss is not being achieved and net gains are needed.

- The policy should put forward management strategies that protect habitat in the first place (prevention of vessel groundings, avoiding release of invasive species, and early detection of invasions, etc.) to avoid costlier and difficult restoration of damaged resources.

- Insure that adaptive management supported by monitoring and applied research is integral to the restoration process.

- The policy could include a decision tree to guide prioritization of restoration projects within the context of climate change and changes in species ranges and habitat condition.

Problem Statement on Project Development and Funding: Inconsistent servicewide project development and inadequate sources of funding for coastal restoration hinder systematic and effective restoration of ocean and coastal habitats. NRPP funding is insufficient and line-item construction funding prioritization does not favor habitat restoration.

Solutions
- Organize a working group to review NPS organizational capacity and develop framework to support servicewide restoration work program for coastal and marine ecological restoration. Institutionalize funding for restoration.

- Develop approach for making ecological restoration projects more competitive under line-item construction and other funding sources, including possible changes to criteria and restoration project scoring.

- Use possible 2010 funding for climate change for competitive project fund for restoration. Revisit timelines for expenditures to accommodate restoration timelines and monitoring.

Problem Statement on NEPA Compliance: NEPA Compliance may not be relevant to changing conditions and time and cost constraints may exceed budgets and timelines.

Solutions

- Establish a working group to propose ways to address time demands and costs of NEPA compliance for restorations projects.

- Broaden CatEx for small-scale ecological restoration projects (in addition to existing categories).

- Investigate use of short form for EAs and provide in-house capacity for completion.

- Consider programmatic EIS similar to coral reef restoration EIS and templates for other coastal and marine habitats.

4. Aquatic Invasive Species

The aquatic invasive species breakout group concluded that the existing NPS Management Policies (Sections 4.4.4, 4.4.4.2, and 4.4.1.3) should be applied in the marine environment, even in the face of climate change. The NPS does not typically apply this policy in the marine environment. The group developed several potential ways to improve the application of these Management Policies.

Problem Statement on Lack of Guidance: There is a lack of systematic guidance and tools to help parks implement the existing NPS Management Policies.

Solutions

- The NPS should convene a working group to develop guidance to assist parks in preparing park-specific or biogeographic invasive species planning documents.

- The guidance would include sections on coordination/collaboration, prevention, early detection/monitoring, rapid response and eradication, long-term control and management, education/outreach, research, and laws/regulations. The guidance could be informed by existing guidance prepared by other entities and should also include:

  - Criteria for determining which aquatic invasive species (current and potential) to manage, risk assessment and decision trees that consider impacts to natural and cultural resources.

  - Examples of what is working, such as agreements, team formation, partnerships, templates of compliance documents and plans, models such as Exotic Plant Management Teams, and public and internal education/outreach.

  - Address vectors (commercial shipping and tourism, commercial fishing, recreational boating, pet industry, etc) systematically, and identify potential control points and mechanisms.

  - Define terms such as non-native, invasive, nuisance, exotic, etc., with enough flexibility to enable management to respond to species and habitat shifts that will occur as a result of climate change.

  - Identify and communicate other sources of information.

Problem Statement on Lack of Science and Scientific Capacity: The NPS lacks scientific basis and scientific capacity (baseline information, inventory and monitoring, impacts, interactions, response, all in light of climate change), which diminishes our credibility.

Solutions

- Compile, synthesize, analyze, and disseminate existing data about aquatic invasives and affected habitats. Sources of existing data include:

- Inventory and Monitoring Networks

- Natural Resource Condition Assessments

- Other sources

- Identify gaps and seek new data/researchers.

  - Regional or national programs should identify research that would be done by CESUs, USGS, etc. and collaborate on writing funding requests (PMIS and external).

  - CESU coordinators and USGS should inventory and disseminate servicewide their respective marine expertise and capacity.

  - Parks can attract researchers by providing boats, housing, mentoring, etc where possible.

  - Agencies and universities should identify incoming threats through modeling (climate change).

  - The NPS Exotic Plant Management Teams and the Biological Resources Management Division may also provide information.

- NRPC should identify and fund key baseline datasets (inventories) for all ocean and coastal parks.

  - The NRPC should obtain benthic habitat mapping and other aquatic data sets on invertebrates, algae, crustaceans, mollusks, marine fish, basic water quality, and other core data sets.

  - NPS should encourage Integrated Ocean Observation System and other data-gathering efforts by NOAA and other agencies to expand into parks.

- The NPS should expand and better use in-house capacity.

  - Parks should obtain and share technical staff to understand the science and translate it to management actions (including details).

  - NPS should train all park staff (e.g., NPS law enforcement, maintenance, and interpretive staff) in ocean and coastal resources, including recognition and reporting of invasive species.

  - The Dive Program should ensure that dive certification refresher requirements include inventory-related work.

  - NPRC should hire or dedicate a scientist at national level to assist parks and regions with marine/aquatic invasives issues/efforts.

Problem Statement on Lack of Public Engagement: The public is not fully informed of and engaged in the impacts of invasive species on park resources.

Solutions

- NPS should incorporate information on invasives into interpretive programs and other types of outreach to increase a public sense of stewardship (e.g., volunteers' monitoring of algae, diving community alerts).

  - Convene a working group of interpreters and invasive species experts to inform and engage the public.

  - Train volunteers in ocean and coastal resources, including recognition and reporting of invasive species.

- Create management plans and heavily advertise public meetings

Problem Statement on Legal Mandates and Enforcement: There is confusion among the NPS and the public about NPS legal mandates and enforcement. For example, the NPS has virtually no regulations about aquatic invasive species in parks.

Solutions
- The NPS should clarify its mandates and servicewide regulations, such as live bait restrictions.

- The NPS should do more law enforcement.

Problem Statement on Partnerships and Collaboration: NPS is not as effective as it could be in partnering and collaborating with other entities.

Solutions
The NPS needs to more effectively understand, define, and communicate our legal jurisdiction/standing, convey our mission, and exchange data in order to improve our collaboration with partners, including interagency and international partners.

- Develop a NPS Director's Order on either climate change and/or ocean management that would clearly affirm that our existing Management Policies and other mandates about invasive species apply in the ocean, coastal and Great Lakes parks.

- Coordinate detection and rapid response among agencies and partners within a geographic area.

- Predict new threats through modeling (e.g., climate change).

- NPS should use the new statute and other available law to work outside park boundaries.

- Share NPS definitions of non-native, exotic, invasive with other entities.

Problem Statement on Ecosystem Resiliency: There is a lack of resiliency of ecosystem process to prevent and/or reduce new invasives.

Solutions
The NPS should conduct and encourage actions that would prevent and/or remove stressors that inhibit the resiliency of park resources.

5. Sediment Management and Coastal Infrastructure
The sediment management and coastal infrastructure breakout group discussed how the NPS will make sound long-term decisions and investments for ocean and coastal areas in the context of climate change and other drivers. Projects related to sediment management, coastal processes, and coastal infrastructure have ramifications beyond the project timeframe or lifecycle, and can greatly influence the public's perception about federal actions. The group identified the development of a consistent process to evaluate competing resource demands as an important goal. Other recommendations include improving relationships with other agencies, developing baseline data and institutional knowledge, and providing improved guidance in some areas (e.g., energy development, beach nourishment, and threatened infrastructure) as goals. The group concluded that NPS needs a paradigm shift in the way that projects are evaluated for funding.

Problem Statement on Evaluation Methods: NPS needs consistent methods to evaluate competing resources and values in the face of climate change, external pressures, and other drivers. How do we decide among protecting natural resources, cultural resources, and visitor enjoyment when a park's enabling legislation and NPS management policies require that we do all of these things? Protecting cultural resources often means impacts and even impairment of a natural process. The reverse is also true; protection of natural processes (e.g., shoreline migration) has impacts on cultural resources. How can superintendents make decisions that can avoid impairment, limit resource management complications, and minimize the chance of litigation?

Solutions

- Understand coastal processes at local and regional scales, and manage for resiliency and adaptability of coastal process-dependent features.

- Develop a decision tree diagram as a method of evaluating when to take action to protect a natural or cultural resource or both. (The minimum tool analysis in the wilderness guidelines could be a basis for this tool.)

- Incorporate analysis of sustainable infrastructure for historic, non-historic, and archaeological resources in existing planning processes, such as GMPs, RSSs, etc.

- Ensure that coastal management is incorporated into a park's planning processes.

- Identify best practices to help develop policy guidance (level 3) or a director's order (level 2).

- Include NRPC and Submerged Resources Center (SRC) resource reviews early in the construction process (before projects go to the DAB). This should be a component of a project's compliance phase and accomplished before a project design is initiated.

- Develop new guidance/template/service expectation that allows a park to meet the intent and requirement of NEPA and Section 106 while reducing the workload required to develop a project EA.

- Insure that park planning scenarios allow for migration of species and habitats (e.g., benthic, water column, beach, dunes).

- Manage systems to perpetuate processes instead of the current status (population or local issue).

Problem Statement on Funding Process: The existing funding process for sediment management, coastal processes, and coastal infrastructure projects is flawed. Projects that are funded describe an action; projects that propose a study do not compete well for funding. Compliance and impact analysis must be valued, required in this process, and funded prior to decisions about construction or along with construction decisions in a phased approach (i.e., projects should be funded with a compliance phase and a construction phase). Flexible decisions about the most appropriate option for mitigation must be a component of the process.

Solutions

- Establish a working group to recommend revisions to the funding process (e.g., Servicewide Comprehensive Call process for Line Item Construction, NRPP, CRPP, etc.). Provide funding for analysis and compliance prior to requesting funding for an action or along with requested action (e.g., construction project).

- Practice adaptive management that allows for iteration between compliance, planning, funding, and implementation. Project funding sources need flexibility to accommodate socio-political, economic, or scientific findings. They must allow consideration for deconstruction and adaptation (may need to reverse an action if it becomes obsolete or counterproductive). Additional guidance is required on how to develop adaptive management techniques or determine adaptive management objectives.

- Streamline all of the information management systems (PMIS, FMSS, ASMIS, LCS, & PEPC).

- Modify Servicewide Comprehensive Call to include a fund for immediate projects.

Problem Statement on Baseline Data: Parks lack baseline data and institutional knowledge. They need additional information about their legal jurisdiction (i.e., location of park boundaries and how to apply them). There is a lack of understanding about potential impacts of park facilities, how to improve the resilience of coastal systems (e.g., habitats, infrastructure) to climate change, how to apply changing storm patterns (e.g., intensities and frequencies), and the impacts resulting from changes in freshwater inputs and throughputs to estuaries and coastal systems.

Solutions
- Develop baseline data and share and enhance institutional knowledge.

- Encourage cultural resource preparation and management prior to and/or after inundation and emergence.

- Improve administrative records. Use software or other electronic process to file/sort/store electronic documents, such as email and correspondence, so that project knowledge is not lost through staff changes.

- Provide information on boundaries to the parks and provide guidance about legal jurisdiction and rights within the park boundary in the water.

Problem Statement on Partnerships: Partnerships with other agencies need to be improved. Infrastructure development on non-park lands (inholdings within park boundary and lands outside of park boundary) affects resources in the park. NPS has insufficient notification and understanding of projects proposed outside of parks that can impact park resources, processes, or infrastructure.

Solutions
- Participate in existing groups and enhance, develop, and participate in partnerships. Additional staff is needed to fully engage with partners (e.g., USACE, USCG, state, regional, local agencies, etc.).

- Develop guidance that explains our legal and service mandates that can be used to educate partners and modify projects to address NPS mandates.

- Develop guidance for parks on the process to engage with other agencies (e.g., USACE, USCG, etc.).

- For any USACE project in or near an NPS unit, the USACE needs to be made aware of the NPS Management Policies that need to be considered and complied with. This may be accomplished through a special use permit.

- Engage early in the process. Develop personal relationships with local and regional planners in order to be more aware of proposed projects.

Problem Statement on NPS Management Policies: The NPS management policies and guidance should provide better information and examples in several areas (i.e., offshore energy development, beach nourishment, threatened existing infrastructure), but maintain flexibility since parks have different levels of coastal development and varied mandates in their enabling legislation.

Solutions

- The following information related to energy development should be included in the management policies:

  - Discuss offshore alternative energy development in ocean section.

  - Include information on siting of alternative energy projects (buffers, off limits, minimum acceptable impacts, etc.).

  - Discuss use of energy to provide power beyond the needs of the park. How does a park provide excess energy developed back to the grid? Should it be encouraged? Does it open a park up to unrealistic expectations of utility companies?

  - Discuss the need to analyze impacts/require NEPA.

  - Discuss the objectives to use alternative energy as a green agency and include in policies where appropriate.

- Other Suggestions for policy revisions

  - Revise cultural resource provisions to incorporate sea level rise or other climate change impacts.

  - Develop guidance that evaluates options to respond to sea level rise and coastal changes (retreat, relocation, beach nourishment, seawalls, and living shorelines). How often will beach nourishment projects be conducted? When is shoreline armoring appropriate at a cultural site if it impacts adjacent coastal habitat? May need to add something in DO-2 to address this issue.

- Proposed Management Policy Revisions

  - 4.8.1.1 Shorelines and Barrier Islands – does not address how we interact with other agencies for proposed structures that will have an impact on a park.

  - 4.8.2.3 Geothermal and Hydrothermal Resources – references the Geothermal Steam Act, but does not state that geothermal leasing is not allowed in parks. This should be included. What about the use of geothermal resources by parks to meet internal needs or objectives? Is this something that should be considered, and if so, under what management conditions would this be acceptable.

  - 8.6.4.2 Utilities – revise section to include language that describes the requirements for director approval for utility corridors (36 CFR Part 14 – Sections 14.70 through 14.78).

  - 9.1.1.5 Siting Facilities to Avoid Natural Hazards – revise section to include the protection of existing infrastructure. Does this apply to a threatened facility? There should be something in the policies related to barrier islands and natural hazards.

  - 9.1.5 Utilities – addresses in-park operations and information only. Revise to consider utilities outside of the park that affect the park resources (such as offshore energy development).

  - 9.1.7 Energy Management – addresses in-park operations and information only. Revise to consider offshore energy development.

  - 9.2 Transportation Systems and Alternative Transportation – only addresses park operations.

  - 10.2 Concessions – addresses the use of alternative energy indirectly, but not meeting the Alternative Energy Objectives of the park.

DAY THREE

During the afternoon of August 27, the workshop participants came together in a plenary session to identify recommendations that cut across all of the topics discussed, and translate the recommendations into next steps or action items.

Cross-Cutting Recommendations

- Clarify and use NPS authorities.

- Apply the NPS Management Policies on the ground.

- Improve administrative processes with NPS

  - Streamline bureaucratic processes (i.e., funding, data, information systems, compliance, reporting).

  - Address inefficient or counterproductive business practices in PEPC, PMIS, and DAB.

  - Reduce funding inequities between construction/rehab and resource/restoration.

- Use the coastal park I&M network structure to enhance collaboration among parks toward addressing common issues and implementing stewardship actions. Obtain sustainable funding to make coastal issues higher priority.

- Obtain, maintain, and use key/baseline data; integrate and share data with other agencies.

- Employ ecosystem management, especially for habitat restoration and fisheries.

- Build ecological resiliency to help parks withstand and adapt to climate change.

- Focus on prevention, early detection, and rapid responses.

- Work with cultural resource experts; cultural resources are linked to natural resource management.

- Include mariculture concerns in the management of fisheries and invasive species.

- Use partnerships where possible; understand the challenges/difficulties working with other agencies.

- Weigh in on external activities that affect parks. Get a seat at the table.

- Explain to the public and other agencies why parks matter.

Turning the Recommendations into Action Items

The workshop participants synthesized the recommendations from the high priority issue breakout groups into the five following overarching recommendations:

Working Groups. The participants suggested that working groups are established to implement the following action items.

1. A working group should address the funding components of restoration and sediment management in the NPS. Revise the Servicewide Comprehensive Call funding mechanism for restoration and sediment management projects (address multi-year funding needs). Allocate more line item construction funding for natural and cultural resource projects (i.e., harmonize funding for line item construction and NRPP). Address the funding of environmental compliance separate from

the project funding.

2. A working group should address water pollution from park facilities and activities, such as septic systems. This group should include representatives from maintenance, natural resources, and cultural resources, and should review processes, evaluate criteria, and recommend revised criteria for funding sources (e.g., line item, rehab-repair, etc.). Give extra weight to known in-park facilities and activities that cause pollution.

3. A working group should develop guidance to assist parks in preparing park-specific or biogeographic planning documents.

4. A working group should develop invasive species guidance to assist parks to bridge the gap between management policies and implementation of the policies.

5. A working group should develop policy and scientific guidance for coastal restoration, including establishing standards. This group should review NEPA compliance procedures and recommend ways to provide more flexibility and speed for habitat restoration by using categorical exclusions and programmatic EISs.

6. A working group should develop a decision tree for sediment management.

7. A working group should continue to clarify NPS authorities and jurisdiction.

8. A working group should develop ecosystem management language appropriate for a DO to move away from management based on single species and/or a snapshot in time. The guidance should contain a list of principles that reflect management for resiliency (e.g., do this, not this; manage for OSY not MSY; remove nonnative species, repatriate extirpated species, etc.).

Director's Order and Reference Manual. Workshop participants also suggested that a Director's Order and Reference Manual (possibly part of the RM 77 series) should be created to provide direction and guidance on the following topics.

1. Marine and coastal ecosystem management principles and implementation.

2. Specific statement that NPS Management Policies on invasive species should be implemented in ocean and coastal parks.

3. Additional guidance for sediment management and coastal infrastructure.

4. Policy and scientific guidance for marine and coastal habitat restoration.

5. Water quality TMDLs and standards – need RM/guidance/handbook to work through system like TMDLs; how NPS implements these processes.

Regulatory Revisions. Workshop participants suggested that the NPS seek regulatory revisions in the following areas.

1. Work with states and USEPA to improve CWA/CZMA anti-degradation water quality regulations/ standards.

2. Work with the USEPA and/or the USCG to improve ballast water regulations and include language that all NPS waters are off-limits to ballast water discharge. Find a way to have our comments be taken seriously.

3. Revise 36 C.F.R. § 2.3 to clarify the applicability of NPS fishing regulations.

4. Revise 36 C.F.R. § 2.1 to clarify that it applies regardless of land ownership.

Legislative Revisions. Workshop participants suggested that the NPS should seek legislative revisions in the following areas.

1. Amendment of Clean Water Act to designate ocean and coastal park waters as Tier III protected waters, if the waters qualify, so that the designation (and anti-degradation protection) is mandatory, rather than at the state's discretion. The legislation could include the sentence "NPS waters shall be afforded the highest level of protection available." A big problem with the current legislation is that states can agree that park waters are pristine and meet the Tier III requirements, but still fail to protect those waters with Tier III designation because of political pressure to avoid limiting nutrient and pollutant discharges into the watershed."

2. Clarification that NPS boundaries should be adjusted so that they include the resources for which the park was established. For example, parks with water depth-based boundaries should be defined by latitude and longitude rather than depth.

3. Amendment of the Submerged Lands Act to address the impacts of sea level rise on state boundaries, federal boundaries, and NPS units.

4. Clarify the goals, purposes, permitted, and non-permitted activities of NPS MPA/marine reserves. Seek legislation to give MPAs more protections; Marine Protection Act is our tool to implement ecosystem management. AND designate wilderness in ocean and coastal parks.

5. Amend the Coastal Zone Management Act to include sediment budget preservation and other park protection components.

Partnerships. Workshop participants suggested that the NPS should strengthen its partnerships and collaboration efforts in the following areas.

1. Develop DOI-USEPA MOU to protect and enhance DOI resource area waters.

2. Implement the recently-signed NOAA-NPS MOU.

3. Include DOI sister agencies (e.g., USFWS) in legislative and regulatory revision efforts.

4. Develop local/regional level partnerships to cooperatively manage local and park water resources.

5. Identify important land parcels to protect through conservation easements.

6. Finalize the national partnership agreement with the USACE.

7. Develop partnerships to improve rapid response/early detection of invasive species.

8. Work with USCG and states to develop geographic response strategies; participate in drills and train for oil spills and prevention.

9. Obtain baseline data from USGS, NOAA, other federal agencies, universities, etc.

10. Remain involved in the Council of Land Management Agency Directors based on November 18, 2003, Pledge for Partnerships.

11. Work in partnerships for ecosystem restoration.

Priorities

- Develop a Director's Order to stimulate and endorse the multiplicity of efforts to protect ocean and coastal park resources (lots of endorsements!).

- Establish no-take areas within each park unit to serve as standards for protection as a component of park research programs (lots of endorsements!).

- Develop a Director's Order firmly stating that NPS Management Policies do apply to marine and coastal resources.

- Develop a national strategy to correct the disparity between marine and terrestrial areas.

- Determine and disseminate NPS jurisdiction and regulatory authorities.

- Engage early and often with all parties and processes affecting marine management. Be assertive and stay at the table.

- Invite others to participate in NPS oceans community of practice through Inside NPS articles and briefings.

- Issue a primer for understanding USACE duties and responsibilities.

- Develop guidelines for coastal ecosystems and processes in light of climate change and manage for resilience.

- Ensure that best available scientific data are used for management actions.

- Designate all park waters as MPAs; implement EO 13158, including law enforcement;

- Designate all park coastal waters as Tier III waters; develop guidance for state and USEPA processes.

- Define healthy fish populations.

- Cooperatively develop benthic habitat inventories for marine parks.

- Streamline and consolidate processes for funding compliance, permitting, and reporting.

- Develop a working group to reform the line-item construction process.

- Disconnect funding for compliance from funding for projects.

- Collect baseline information on coastal processes, resources, and infrastructure in parks.

- Develop a mechanism to evaluate competing cultural and natural resource projects.

- Use a systematic approach to build the NPS ocean program.

NPS 999/102099, May 2010